BORN TO LIVE

by Peter Yarrell

Torn Curtain Publishing
Wellington, New Zealand
www.torncurtainpublishing.com

2nd Edition © Copyright 2022 Peter Yarrell. All rights reserved.

ISBN Softcover 978-0-473-63349-3

ISBN EPub 978-0-473-63350-9

No portion of this book may be reproduced, stored in a retrieval system or transmitted in any form or by any means – electronic, mechanical, photocopy, recording or otherwise – except for brief quotations in printed reviews or promotion, without prior written permission from the author.

Details of events, locations and interactions are included according to the author's best recollection at the time of writing. Some names and identifying details of people described in this book have been altered to protect their privacy.

Unless otherwise noted, all scripture is taken from the Holy Bible, New International Version®, NIV®. Copyright © 1973, 1978, 1984, 1985, 2011 by Biblica, Inc.™ Used by permission of Zondervan. All rights reserved worldwide.

Cover design by Alexander Lloyd. Used with permission of Tour of New Zealand.

Internal design by Carolyn Campbell.

Photography by Dr. Newell Grenfell and Scottie Taylor. Used with permission.

Cataloguing in Publishing Data
    Title: *Born to Live* (2nd edition).
    Author: *Peter Yarrell*
    Subjects: Sports performance, Cycling, Coaching, Spirituality and faith.

A copy of this title is held at the National Library of New Zealand.

"I have enjoyed knowing Peter Yarrell for forty years and have rarely known anyone as positive, exuberant, exciting and exhilarating! The many different and often remarkable spokes of his wheel find their security in the stabilising hub of his relationship with God, without which you will not understand him. Encouraging, inspiring, sobering and challenging are all words I use to describe this book."

—Charles Price, Toronto, Canada

"The Tour of New Zealand has not had a start-line without me on it; yes, all six tours! Here on the start line of *Born to Live* through to the finish line, I have been equally challenged and absorbed."

—Rod Oram, Business Journalist, New Zealand

"In this book you will take a 'virtual ride' through the remarkable life of Peter Yarrell. Prepare to be surprised, amazed and inspired, as you journey with Peter towards his very personal 'finish line'."

—Mike Pollok, Managing Director, Ricoh

To all the amazing people (and my Coach), who ride with me on the Tour of Life.

and

To all our competitors who ran, cycled or kayaked in:

The AMP City of Christchurch Multi Sport Race
The Queen Charlotte Classic
The Lochmara Lodge Half Marathon
The Tour of New Zealand

and have selflessly raised over two million dollars so far to support the work of our events' charity partners.

FOREWORD

I first met Peter and Jilly Yarrell through their effervescent daughter Angie on a trip to Picton. My purpose was to visit the crash site on Mt Robertson of a Sounds Air Flight in which I lost, at age twenty-six, my beloved (and married for just one day) little sister Katrina and her husband in 1996.

Years later, Peter invited my husband Kieran and me to ride the *Tour of New Zealand*. Anyone who has ridden 'The Tour' with Peter will know that it's not really a choice. It's one of those commitments you can't evade because of the awe and respect in which you hold the one who is goading you, albeit with a façade of optionality! Peter's urging and enthusiasm can be as infuriatingly overwhelming and inconvenient as it is irresistible. In a way, this is analogous for my own relationship with God.

Peter epitomises the joy to be found in taking risks, trusting that God will provide, and simply making life better for others. His endless energy and enthusiasm is a virtuous cycle of giving (and so receiving) joy. Part of Peter's success in helping people is because he genuinely doesn't appear to seek recognition. Human desire for power and status often gets in the way of building teams that can truly change outcomes for the better. Peter seemingly lacks that selfish need, or perhaps he succeeds in suppressing it. Peter's legacy is in the people he's raised funds for, helped, listened to and 'picked up'.

His stories are so relatable because they describe the struggles we all share: human vulnerability, temptation, success and failure. This is a book to be read, enjoyed and reflected upon. You may even find yourself asking some honest questions. His story is an example of a lifetime of generosity, and it has touched Kieran and me and our kids, many times. I am eternally grateful for Peter Yarrell's relentless bullying of this ordinary non-athlete into the ride of my life (not once, but four times!) The fun, pleasure and pain is just one part of it. Taking a full eight days out of a normal schedule to rediscover what really matters, among wonderful people who exude consideration for their fellow riders—well, let's just say it's more than worth it. There is deep satisfaction in riding day after day, when you think you have nothing left to give from the 100 kilometre-plus ride of the previous day, only to discover that *plus est en vous* (more is in you).

This brings me back to our first reason for meeting, and why I resonate so much with *Born to Live*. The crash site on Mt Robertson is a beautiful and peaceful place where the view across the sea to infinity seems fitting, an appropriate place for Katrina and Liam to move to the next 'stage' while remaining forever young, beautiful and in love, even if the timing was seemingly inappropriate for those they left on the hill climb. There is no question the pair of them allow me to draft off them still, as did Pete when we cruised into Te Kuiti on a very bleak and rainy stage of the Tour in 2017. I'm personally very clear who the lead rider actually is though. If you haven't already decided who yours is, this book will help you decide.

It's a privilege to know Pete and Jilly. But for my own tragedy, I may never have met them.

Leonie Guiney

Peter, Leonie and husband Kieran Guiney, prior to the start of the first Tour of New Zealand in 2012.

Nine years later, Leonie takes on the Crown Range on Stage 2 of the 2021 Tour of New Zealand.

CONTENTS

FOREWORD		i
PREFACE		v
PROLOGUE		1
STAGE 1	My Coach sets me up on my bike	3
STAGE 2	An early attack	7
STAGE 3	Fighting mental battles on and off the bike	10
STAGE 4	Self-inflicted pain by not listening to my Coach	14
STAGE 5	A serious climb	20
STAGE 6	My first break and some downhill runs	30
STAGE 7	A crash in the peloton	36
STAGE 8	Which route?	40
STAGE 9	Road works. Slow down!	47
STAGE 10	Changing gears	52
STAGE 11	The mountain stages	55
STAGE 12	Team tactics	65
STAGE 13	Back to basics	82
STAGE 14	Downhill and a tail wind	85
STAGE 15	Supporting each other	90
STAGE 16	A very high mountain road	98
STAGE 17	Preparation for the penultimate stage	104
STAGE 18	A wrong turn and a lesson hopefully learned	106
STAGE 19	A bypass, but not on the road	110
STAGE 20	The valley of the shadow of death	114
STAGE 21	A face-to-face with my Coach	125
STAGE 22	Who is your 'Lead out' rider?	132
STAGE 23	The crash every rider fears	136
STAGE 24	Tandem power for the asking	144
ACKNOWLEDGEMENTS		151

PREFACE

We have about 26,000 days (more or less) allotted us to live on planet Earth. Even so, we're always just one breath away from dying!

After birth we have, obviously, a one hundred percent chance of death.

There are many ways of understanding the meaningfulness (or not) of life, but from my observations, there are really only two stand-out options:

1. We can use up our time on earth with a rat-in-a-cage philosophy. Life is simply a fight for survival in a cage called Earth. Beating others to the food and having a better nest and rest at night are the overarching objectives. Luck is the game-changer for the better or the game-wrecker for the worse.

or:

2. Life has purpose. A guiding hand steers us and equips us with the discipline of a good conscience. We soon realise life is a gift that if given away, is discovered in even greater abundance.

So … are we born to die, or are we born to live?

In 1964, at the age of twenty, I read a book that I felt came by courier directly from a post office in heaven addressed personally to me. It was a life story. One half of me could scarcely bear to read it, and the other half clung to every word. It was the first edition of *Devil at my Heels*, by Louis Zamperini.

Captured by the Japanese after the B24 bomber he was a tail gunner in crashed into the ocean, Louis and two airmen spent the next forty-seven days in a life raft, adrift in the Pacific. One of his crew had to be buried at sea. After Louis' rescue (and capture), the Japanese realised he was no ordinary prisoner of war. Louis had represented the United States of America in the 1936 Berlin Olympics where he'd come fifth in the 5000-metre race. As a United States champion, he was a big find for the Japanese war machine. This made him the target of almost unreadable torture until the liberation by Allied forces in 1945.

His journey into faith was accompanied by nightmarish treatment as perpetrators aimed to destroy him from the inside-out. After the war, however, Louis had a transformational encounter with God at a Billy Graham crusade. The effect of this encounter was so strong that Louis found himself able to return to Japan where he faced many of his captors and shared with them the forgiveness he had received in his new-found faith.

Reading Louis' book breathed into me admiration, not only for Zamperini himself, but also for the God who had loved and rescued him.

Twenty years later I had the amazing opportunity of meeting Zamperini after randomly picking up a newspaper which gave details of his impending visit to Christchurch, New Zealand. Louis was scheduled to visit the city for two days during a ski holiday, and when I reached out to him, he said he'd enjoy meeting us and some friends over dinner. That evening, eye to eye, I was honoured to tell him of the powerful influence his book and life story had on me. That's when I realised that his Coach had become my Coach too!

That evening, Louis humbly and thoughtfully shared his heart with us. It was crazy! We were sitting in a restaurant in the company of this legend of a man who had so much he could brag about, but this plainly didn't even occur to him. He had our group laughing as he spoke of how he'd recently been appointed part-time youth pastor of the Hollywood Presbyterian Church. He was sixty-five at the time, and I guess I looked surprised.

"The kids say that when I can no longer do a handstand on my skateboard and then ride it down the church ramp, they'll dump me as their youth pastor," he told us. I realised at that moment that Louis was no aging war veteran. His style, fitness, athletic body and youthful spirit had no bounds.

In writing *Born to Live*, I am so inspired by the Louis Zamperinis of this world. The Hollywood film *Unbroken* depicts his war years, though not his faith years. Nevertheless, it's certainly worth watching.

I refer often to the Spirit of God as my Coach. The tragic denigration of the name and person of Jesus Christ is at the top of any scale of hate speech use. It never ceases to amaze me how the angry, frustrated and self-absorbed, who claim there is no God, resort in times of trouble to cursing the very God they believe is non-existent. In case you too have been contaminated by this, I have chosen to call the Spirit of God, my Coach.

In these pages are stories I have recounted as accurately as possible, although the conversations are recalled from memory and many actual names have been long forgotten. In this case, I have used random names to imbue the conversations with meaning.

We could rationalise every bump and blessing along the road as coincidence upon coincidence. Conversely, the life story you are about to read may give you a reason to think, ponder, and plan—to 'climb on your bike and make it to the start'. I have no monopoly on the Coach. He has been at His work for the last 2000-years plus, in people far more worthy than me. But with my Coach, 'worthy' doesn't seem to matter.

I have called each chapter in this book a 'stage'. In a multi-day bike race or ride, each day is defined as a stage. As you ride with me along the course of my life, I hope you will see that life is made up of stages from which we learn and grow.

In 2012 I had the privilege of planning and organising an eight-day multi-stage bike race we named *The Tour of New Zealand*. It's a biennial *Tour de France*-style event for riders who love the intrigue of competition, but who also carry a passion to raise money for their chosen charity.

Like the *Tour of New Zealand* or the *Tour de France*, living will make you face an extraordinary journey, one that has been planned by the organisers to test your limits. Each stage requires skills and fitness to compete and complete, and every stage has its own set of challenges. Unexpected cold, rain and wind, a puncture, a crash, a train stopped on a railway crossing, a wrong turn, a fellow team member letting you down, a mechanical failure, a lack of fluids or food, sickness, a course change or cramp—everything is a possibility in the context of our lives, just as in a multi-stage bike race.

Imagine with me that you're enjoying a morning coffee with someone like Chris Froome, four-time winner of the *Tour de France*. Fresh in his mind is the Tour he has just won. You feel you almost know him as you have watched, read, and imagined the intrigue, the pain, the critical decisions and the mistakes he made on this epic twenty-four-day race across France.

The insights he gained, how he dealt with bike and body, would make for a riveting twenty minutes.

After each of my twenty-four stages in the Tour of Life, you will read of crashes, punctures, and my misreading the course map. I will share with you my thoughts along the way, as well as the actions I took.

When people of faith on life's journey ignore the directions of the marshal, or puncture a tyre, or experience a mechanical failure, or crash, they are often mocked and judged. What the judgemental do not understand is that both Coach and support crew expect amongst their riders many crashes and punctures along the *Tour of Life*. They are assigned twenty-four hours a day to get the bike sorted and rider patched up so that he or she can rejoin the peloton, repaired and restored.

My story is about a life often punctuated by what some may call coincidences, and others would call miracles. Perhaps there is a mixture of both; I leave that for you to decide.

You will see that being 'born to live' takes you into a battle. On the start line of a bike race every friend racing with you turns inevitably from buddies into competitors. At the sound of the starter's siren, your relationship with each other suddenly changes. You will do all in your power to ride away from your best friends in order to win.

Thankfully, in life we don't compete against our fellow 'riders'.

However, when I chose the *Born to Live* life, I was surprised to find a battle ignited within me. Powers of darkness showed up to fight the new spirit within me. Every thought, every action and every motivation came under a searchlight. All my intentions to live a good life seemed to get a 'fail' mark under the scrutiny of the high standards of my heavenly Coach … or so I felt. But this Coach was different. He was there alongside me, never to condemn, but only to encourage, restore, and teach me life lessons that would protect me and take me places I never could have dreamed about. I had entered a battle, not against competitors in a bike race. I was in a fight between being born to live, or born to die. And it became incredibly exciting as the stages unfolded. It's life and death stuff.

Join me on the start line.

BORN TO LIVE

*"Everyone comes naked from
their mother's womb,
and as everyone comes, so they depart.*

*They take nothing from their toil
that they can carry in their hands."*

ECCLESIASTES 5:15

PROLOGUE

At the beginning of a multi-day bike tour, a 'prologue' is often used to set the scene for the stages ahead and introduce riders to each other.

Wellington's Evening Post numbered the crowd that gathered each night at the rugby ground, Athletic Park, at around forty thousand. It was 1959, and American evangelist, Billy Graham, challenged his audience. "Follow your own self-centred ways," he said, "but remember, *There is a way that seems right to a man, but the end thereof is death.*" He quoted the proverb from the bible, then added, "... or invite Jesus Christ to be your light and friend, and discover a life journey that will place His hand in yours."

I listened intently.

"Jesus said *I have come to give life to you in all its abundance,*" the young evangelist proclaimed. "If you know deep down that this is your day of discovery, quietly walk forward across the grass. We have folks here that will pray for you and help you begin your journey."

I sat in a compromised seat. Beside me was my bike-racing buddy, Des Thompson. I glanced at him and weighed up my options. I squirmed. A tug of war raged. What would Des think? Did that matter? *Just walk,* I told my legs. *No don't. Yes, do!* I hung between the two options as Billy Graham invited everyone one last time.

"This is a day that will give you a new destiny," he declared.

I found myself thinking, *Just do it.* Not daring to glance beside me at

Des, I walked forward. I felt like a baby taking step number one, the first of the millions of steps ahead in its lifetime.

Without a step one, I figured there could never be a step two…

As our bus headed home, Des turned to me and asked, "So do you think if an atomic bomb falls out of the sky on the way home, you will die and go to heaven now?"

I did not have a clue how to answer him.

MY THOUGHTS

The nervous step of faith I had taken that afternoon and the battle I had gone through to get my legs walking across the rugby park began to make more sense. I had been given, so to speak, the lightest, fastest racing bike ever to ride the stages of life, but I didn't realise it.

C.S. Lewis quoted Francis Thompson when he called God's Spirit 'the Hound of Heaven'. This Hound didn't run out of puff until it hunted C.S. Lewis down. The same Hound of Heaven had validated my entry into the *Tour of Life*. Now I just had to clip my shoes onto the pedals and start the tour. Where it would lead, I didn't know.

The Hound that had hunted me down somehow morphed into my Coach for the stages of the race ahead. I was about to go into some high-altitude training.

STAGE 1

My Coach sets me up on my bike

An invitation to accompany a student to Wellington's Queen Margaret College ball of 1960 turned out to have major ramifications. I fell in love. Susan captivated me. She was a sincere, gentle, loving girl with caring parents who always warmly welcomed me to their home.

My father disapproved and completely misread the situation. Summoning my older brother, Robert, and I, he handed us tickets to leave on the next sailing of the passenger liner *Southern Cross*, destination England. I was seventeen and Robert was twenty-one. My father wanted us both out of town.

With a young, aching heart, I waved goodbye to Susan. It was January 1962 when the *TS Southern Cross* gave five forlorn blasts on her ship's horn, then slid quietly away from Kings Wharf. Faithfully waving to me from the wharf, Susan slowly and painfully disappeared from my sight. I couldn't hide from my brother my wet cheeks. With blurred eyesight and my emotions torn apart, I headed to our six-berth cabin. It was the start of a five-week sea journey to the other side of the world.

My faith was ever-present, but barely visible to an onlooker. Life in London began with a battle both within and without. To my seventeen-year-old, grappling-to-grow-up brain, London was overpowering. But I had to make it. Deep down I believed that whatever doesn't kill you only makes you stronger. Thankfully, there seemed to be a gentle hand on my shoulder steering me into opportunities and life lessons, sometimes into and then out of trouble, to grow me up.

The Overseas Visitors' Club at Earls Court was a meeting place for many, and working in the kitchen put bread on the table and money in the landlord's bank account. Dishwashing for sixteen hours a day at thirty pence an hour balanced the books, and so dishwashing it was. That was until I unknowingly tripped myself up.

"I am so broke," I announced one day over our ten-minute staff morning tea break. "I would do anything for some extra cash."

Thinking nothing more, I was surprised when an older South African edged up to me as I returned to my dishwashing station, and in a quiet, friendly voice suggested, "If you really want some extra cash, I can help you."

This sounded like the break I was looking for, and I asked him what my job would be. He said we could meet after work in the club lounge and he would explain. He seemed very caring, and I thought how good it would be to perhaps get paid fifty pence an hour rather than the thirty pence I was currently earning.

I arrived early for our meeting to find Oscar was already seated by the fireplace in the dimly lit lounge.

"Hi Oscar. I'm really excited about our conversation earlier today," I said. "I need a break. My pay hardly sorts the rent!"

Ignoring my enthusiasm, Oscar didn't choose to talk about the job directly.

"You are young to be so far from home. New Zealander, eh?"

He said he had friends from New Zealand and could pick the Kiwi accent.

"I'm really keen to hear about your job for me, Oscar. You said you're in advertising. What's involved?"

"Well, it's a bit complicated," he replied. "I can put it this way. Could you come home with me tomorrow night? You can stay overnight if you want to. I will take photos of you. It is very lucrative."

"Really? This sounds interesting," I replied guardedly. "But what do I do? Advertising what?"

I felt suddenly uneasy. On first acquaintance, Oscar seemed a caring sort of person, but now he looked uncomfortable and short on words.

"How does that earn me money?" I asked.

Oscar explained that he lived with some other men and they had a house nearby. But he plainly didn't want to answer my question.

"Why don't you just come with me and I will tell you when we get home," he suggested.

Alarm bells rang. "No, Oscar. You tell me now. Are you into advertising?"

Oscar looked away. "Okay," he said. "We will take photos of you naked, and you will earn lots of money. You said you would do anything for money, right?"

"Did you say *naked*?" I stared at him in amazement. I was repulsed.

Finding my voice, I said the first thing that came into my head.

"I am a Christian, and I don't believe this conversation!"

As cool and as smooth as a snake, Oscar replied. "I am a Christian too!"

I could not think clearly enough to find more words. Should I punch this predator? I leapt to my feet, turned, and made my way to the pay office at the club. Handing in my notice, I asked to be paid up for my work, then left my dishwashing job at the Overseas Visitors' Club.

MY THOUGHTS

My Coach throws me in at the deep end. In a way, the lightness, speed, and opportunity a racing bike affords is almost intoxicating. The power and agility must be well-controlled, or the bike could send me flying off a sharp bend to my death. As a child, I felt my earthly father had little love for me, and the heated arguments my parents indulged in resulted in insecurity. My lack of confidence in myself could have led me in the wrong direction that day, but my Coach protected me when He gave me the idea to find out what was on Oscar's mind first. The thought still makes me shudder!

STAGE 2

An early attack

Life was about to get a little violent.

The New Cross swimming pool in south-west London advertised for a lifeguard. The bronze medallion I had achieved on the beaches of Wellington got me the job, but as it turned out, not the skills to hold the job down.

It wasn't just my idea to order six trouble-makers out of the pool. Standing beside me was the no-nonsense lifeguard who dealt with disorder. You didn't argue with him. Physically he was a mountain of a man, a semi-professional boxer.

"That language doesn't have a home in this pool, so get out, get dressed, and get lost!" he shouted across the pool to half a dozen teenagers. The gang had taken over a diving board and were bouncing on it dangerously, terrifying the other swimmers and yelling obscenities at them. Within five minutes they were dressed. They leered, cursed and swore at Mr Muscle and me as they shuffled outside and into a fifty-metre narrow alleyway that led to a quiet road that ran down to a second pool and the laundry.

With the troublemakers gone, I gathered a stack of wet towels using my arms as a human forklift, then headed off to the pool laundry. I was surprised when I walked straight into the gang lingering outside the pool entrance. Confronted with the option of a quick back-pedal into the safety of the pool or walking along the alleyway I thought, *Just walk past them.* They were huddled together lighting up cigarettes, and I figured if I walked quickly I could reach the top of the alleyway and the safety of a quiet but public street.

I had only ever witnessed one street fight in New Zealand, and it was ugly. Like a fire, it had generated its own storm winds and went from bad to worse.

I hurried past the six teenagers and headed up the alleyway.

I was conscious they were on my case, stalking me, intimidating me, walking close behind me. One of them flicked his foot against mine trying to ankle tap me to the ground. I stumbled, conscious I was unable to defend myself with my arms full of damp, smelly towels.

Turning my head I muttered a throwaway line, thinking it would be enough to cause them to back up. "Do that again and I will drop you!"

I quickened my pace to reach the top of the alleyway and turned to walk the last fifty metres down the quiet side street and to the safety of the pool laundry. I realised later that my threat probably stalled them enough to give me time to reach the top of the alleyway.

Out of the corner of my eye I noticed the gang leader drop his swimming togs on the tray of a small truck. That was my only warning. His fist landed its first blow between my eyes. Blood dripped from my nose, and it was all on. The next forty seconds or so were a blur as the gang did their best to knock me to the ground. Miraculously, I stayed upright, nose bleeding, clothes ripped, and dazed, but still on my feet. I knew their plan would be to kick me black and blue if they could get me down.

It was over as quick as it had started. The gang fled. Stunned, I left the towels strewn across the pavement and ducked into the entrance and safety of the laundry complex I'd been heading toward as a small group of patrons gave me a cheer.

Taking a breath and watching out for further trouble, I returned to the street and gathered the towels. I was amazed no one helped me. Even the laundry staff showed no sign of compassion or support as I handed them the splattered towels.

I wondered how long it would be before the gang would return to continue where they'd left off.

The hop season was about to get into full swing. The farmer on the end of the phone promised me basic accommodation in Kent, south east of London and a six-day working week with ten-hour days for a six-week season. It sounded like a great plan. Hopefully country living would be a little kinder to me.

MY THOUGHTS

The night after the fight and my check-up for a broken nose, I tried to slide into sleep, but the action of the day was still buzzing around my head. My 'crash off the bike' could have been much worse, and I realised that I needed a lot more wisdom in this race to keep me out of trouble ahead. I promised myself I'd engage my brain before I engaged my mouth. I felt very thankful to my Coach for what seemed like wisdom from above.

STAGE 3

Fighting mental battles on and off the bike

I had no idea where Kent was, but I had my racing bike, a pack and a map, and reckoned on a three to four-hour ride depending on how lost I got on the way. I was fascinated to pass handsome old country pubs, some with crude signs hanging on their balconies that simply said 'No Gypsies'. Coming from New Zealand, I wasn't sure who or what gypsies were, but decided if they were real people, it was quite unfair they couldn't go to a pub.

Indeed, the farmer was right with his term 'basic' accommodation. I found a cottage with three bedrooms, a double mattress on the floor of each room, a rough kitchen, one toilet, one shower, and a small sitting room. The six wooden chairs doubled as dining and lounge chairs.

A Kiwi accent interrupted my thoughts. "Hi! I am John Ormond from Gisborne. You here to pick hops too?"

It was a bonus to have another Kiwi to work with, and I introduced myself.

Looking at the other hop-pickers, it was very apparent to John and myself that we were the best choice for room-mates. We threw down our sleeping bags to claim our bedroom and unhitched our back packs that contained the basics for six weeks. The farmer's wife promised she would wash our clothes once a week, and directed us to a nearby shop where we could buy basics.

The other members of our picking gang looked pretty formidable. They were more interested it seemed, in the amount of beer they drank after work, than being personable and friendly by day. The conversations by night centred around these South Africans outdoing each other, telling us bragging stories of their hurtful actions around race and colour they either didn't respect or habitually abused. They noticed I didn't enjoy their stories and that I didn't swear.

"Why don't you swear?" Ray, the tallest of them, looked amused by me. "Come on, Pete. Swear just once for us!"

Ray had the best job of us pickers. He drove the tractor up and down the rows whilst John and I stood on a long platform above his head slashing the vines with a sharp knife attached to our wrists. We then flicked the vines behind us, stacking them in layers along the tray of the specially modified tractor. If Ray was moody for any reason he would drive too fast, and John and I couldn't cut quick enough, missing some vines. We would yell at him to slow down. Unless it really got dangerously stupid, I just hung on and said nothing more. After listening to his stories about South Africa it seemed wiser to play his games, knowing that at the end of the day and after a few beers he would settle down.

In our lunch break one warm spring afternoon, Ray opened up the conversation. "We have never met anyone who doesn't swear and blaspheme. You are strange, Pete!"

This trio had worked together in South Africa and were I guessed, aged about twenty-five. John and I discovered they'd been kicked out of South Africa for seriously mistreating people.

"You are a Christian, we know. Come on man, just one swear word," Ray persisted.

I hadn't told them I had a faith, but I also hadn't hidden it. I would read my tattered travel bible in our very basic lounge some evenings. I felt that my faith was the elephant in the room, but nobody commented.

"You can do it! Just say—," and they chose some vile blasphemy.

"Let me tell you about my London fight." I changed the subject and got their attention. Fights interested them, and they listened attentively. I told them that I felt some angel had swooped in and rescued me.

"The man believes in angels too!" Ray mocked.

For the first time in my life, at the age of seventeen, I tried to explain my faith. They were sort of interested, and I knew they liked working with me on the hops. Their acceptance of me as a fellow hop worker was important. Ray and his friends had only just arrived from South Africa, and I wondered what they had done to the 'blacks' that got them deported.

My explanation of God and my faith was mocked and questioned—and rightly so. My faith gave me a purpose and energy to work hard and laugh a lot, and I think they could see that. But in their eyes it was a faith without reason. As I explained what I could, it was obvious even to me that I was completely out of my depth. However, unbeknown to my three South African fellow hop pickers that day, they'd initiated in me a hunger for credibility.

The peacefulness and beauty of the English countryside and working day after day amongst the rows and rows of hop vines, did wonders for me. The early starts were acknowledged every morning with shrill birdsong and budding flower perfumes I had never noticed in New Zealand. London seemed distant, and all the action of the previous weeks was safely tucked away, now only in my occasional thoughts. Ray and his friends never again asked me to swear, and we became good mates.

With the hop picking season over, I headed back to London for a stint at chauffeur-driving the rich and the famous around the West End.

MY THOUGHTS

My year in England was truly a university of hard knocks. It was a phrase my father had used when he'd given my brother and me the tickets to go to 'the other end of the planet'.

I felt a hand on my shoulder always guided me, rescued me, and provided for me, not least with lessons. This stage taught me to toughen up, to realise how much stronger I needed to be if I was ever to contribute speed in the peloton.

STAGE 4

Self-inflicted pain by not listening to my Coach

In February 1963, the *Southern Cross* returned me to the same Wellington wharf as my brother and I had departed from thirteen months previously. Robert decided to stay on in London. Within days of arriving home I began to feel seriously melancholy. London was calling me back. I now looked at Wellington through different eyes and wondered why I'd ever returned. I had one thought in front of mind—go back to London—take the next ship and replenish my bank account.

As I searched the papers for a ship back to London, I noticed in the Evening Post newspaper an advertisement for a job with a television station. It got my heart thumping.

Unexpectedly, I was selected to become a television news reporter. In my head, it was a job I really wanted, but deep down in my heart I felt I was going into a world that wasn't quite me.

My first day on the job with Wellington's TV One had me working as an understudy to the chief news reporter. I had to learn how to type, construct stories, interview, and work with the announcers and recording suites. I wasn't exactly the best choice for the job. My English teacher four years previously had berated me in front of my fifth form class, assessing an essay I had written, and sharing the opinion that I was a total failure at written expression!

I had a lot to learn.

Derek, my boss and chief reporter, kept having to push his glasses back up the bridge of his nose as he wrote his stories. He gave me guidelines, then let me write. We would film a story together and I would write a voiceover to accompany the pictures. Sound on film was very expensive and the TV station engaged the National Film Unit if they wanted that service. It was mainly a silent film production—we directed the cameraman for the shots we needed, write the voiceover commentary, then a newsreader would record the words onto a tape, and we would next sync the words and film together once we had edited the film.

After a month I was given a taxi chit book. Now we had wheels, and with a cameraman, we set off on 'the day mission'. Our job was to find two local stories the TV station could show that night under the segment *Wellington Today*.

My first important assignment took me to Wellington airport to interview American jazz legend, Louis Armstrong. My first impressions of him were of his heavily scarred lips and raspy, gravel voice. I felt overawed by the moment and worked hard at asking questions and recording answers that would fit the evening news story of Louis' arrival in our country. It was surreal to be meeting people I never dreamed I'd have the privilege of talking with.

Later that day, the cameraman and I were dropped off by a tug to board a US Navy warship as it steamed across Wellington harbour. This time, our assignment was to capture the welcome of the ship's crew to New Zealand.

Sometimes we were not back to the studio until 4 p.m. The news story had to be recorded by 5.30 p.m., ready to be run at 6.15 p.m. In that time, I would edit the film, write the story, then race across to the recording suite, cue the newsreader as it was recorded to sync the story with the film, then run back to the station in time to give it to the projectionist who'd put it on air.

Being the apprentice, I had to have my work checked by the sub-editor, and if he thought it wasn't quite right, he'd make alterations. This made life very difficult, as the sub-editor went to the pub every night at 5 p.m. (The pubs shut at 6 p.m. in 1963). By the time he returned there were only minutes until the story went to air. If he made changes I found myself panicking, to the point where I could make mistakes.

Weeks later, after filming some university students on a capping stunt trying unsuccessfully to paddle a bathtub across Evans Bay, I caught the last train of the evening for the forty-five-minute journey home. It was 11.30 p.m. when the train departed the station. I was tired, and the mesmeric rumble of the electric train sent me to sleep.

To my horror, I awoke to find the empty train leaving the final station for the return journey back to Wellington. I leapt to my feet, grabbing my briefcase. Half asleep, I flung the door open that links the carriages. Standing on the handrail bar between carriages, I went to throw my briefcase on to the rapidly-disappearing station platform and prepared to leap off between the carriages as the train accelerated out of the station.

An image from nowhere filled my mind. In an instant, it took me back to age seven when I had stupidly leapt off a high branch of a tall tree, believing that the lower branches would cushion my fall. I left hospital three days later, having had the smashed bones in my right arm plastered back into place.

The memory sat vividly in front of me at that moment, so I clambered back down off the safety handrail, returned to the carriage, and pulled the emergency stop lever. The train came to a screeching halt and the doors opened automatically. I jumped down onto the end of the platform as the guard ran towards me. "I'm so sorry. I didn't see you in the carriage before we left the platform," he apologised.

I was relieved he wasn't angry, as the emergency stop lever had a huge warning in red saying that misuse of the emergency stop would be met with a fine that was bigger than my bank balance. He apologised a second time, and I retrieved my brief case and fumbled for the keys to my motorbike with a shaking hand.

That short ride home gave me time to think. The horror three days in Lower Hutt Hospital twelve years earlier had a purpose I had never considered.

My nineteen years on the planet could have ended that night. I didn't know then that a week later I would no longer be a TV reporter. I was about to be sacked!

The chief reporter greeted me on the following Monday morning with a message: "The manager wants to talk to you in his office now."

I sat in the chair opposite the TV station manager's desk. "Peter, as you know, you are our latest addition to the news team. Last week an experienced Canadian journalist applied for a job with us." The manager looked anxious, and I wondered where the conversation was going.

"There isn't room for the three of you, so I have decided that you will have to go. We can give you a job as a floor manager for productions…" he added quickly.

I will never forget the sensation that came with that news. For the first time ever, I felt the blood in my fingertips throbbing, really pulsating. I just sat and stared at him.

As I stood to leave he said, "Oh, by the way, my secretary, Helen, wants to have a few moments with you. She is just down the corridor in the tearoom."

Helen was sipping on her coffee in the almost-empty staff tearoom. She seemed to expect my visit.

"Peter, I know your news, and I am sorry." I liked Helen, and we had chatted often. "Normally, I would never get involved," she said, "but I just have to this time. I have enjoyed you working with us here, Pete. You are always so willing. In fact, you are like fresh air around the place. But to be honest, you don't quite fit."

Helen's voice was full of compassion and empathy. "Television staff have a common problem," she continued. "They will elbow you out of line, talk behind your back, and clamber over anyone to climb the tree. I can tell that you are too good for this media world. Your style just doesn't fit here, and as gutted as you will be, there is a future for you that will take you way further than you would ever go working here."

Her words hung in the air, so I let them slowly sink in.

"Can I make you a coffee?" Helen asked.

"Not now, but thanks, Helen," I replied.

A door had slammed shut in my face. The role in TV productions wasn't 'me'. When I returned to my desk, Derek, the chief reporter who had taught me, was nowhere to be seen. I felt I was beginning to flourish in my writing and interviewing skills, and wanted to talk to him. I was disappointed he had purposely left the office, not wanting to front up. I had questions, and I needed answers. He had taught me well, but he'd never allowed himself to be a friend.

I gathered my pens and notebooks. Feeling foolish and lonely and rejected, I found myself reflecting on the day I'd applied for the job. I had to admit to myself that I was aware of push-back from my Coach, but I so wanted the role (and, I guessed, the glamour of being a television journalist) that I closed my ears to Him. When I first went for the job, the station manager had seemed so unwilling to give it to me, and only by persistence, possibly verging on manipulation, I had talked him into signing me on.

Wellington that day seemed very cold. The southerly wind was bitter, and the skies grey. *What's next?* I pondered, as I walked through the almost deserted railway station that mid-afternoon.

MY THOUGHTS

I'd pursued this glamour job with a lot of energy, which in hindsight I should have conserved. Being in that job felt like leading the pack to win a mid-race sprint, when deep down I should have been conserving energy and obeying the words from my Coach through my headphones over the team radio. The adulation and cheering of the crowd negated His wisdom, and I would pay the price at the finish, exhausted and disappointed. However, again the Coach used my misspent enthusiasm to teach me a lesson I needed to learn, on a relatively flat stage early in the tour.

STAGE 5

A serious climb

In the 1960s, the New Zealand government supported its military partners in the Vietnam War. Our nation required recruits, and so had installed a ballot system that took the birth date of every nineteen-year-old male and put these into a Lotto-style number draw. If your birthday was randomly selected, no questions asked—you were marched off and trained to fight.

"I don't believe it!" I told my brother-in-law, Craig. "Are you sure?"

We were in the middle of a game of table tennis, and I was about to serve. I froze.

"Yes," he said. "You're off to the army for national service, Peter. The annual birthday lottery turned up your date, the 11th of January. The list was in this morning's paper."

Craig was a volunteer engineer in the army which he referred to sarcastically as the *Sons of Fun*.

"You've been conscripted into the army. You'll probably end up in Vietnam trying to shoot Viet Cong."

This had to be a bad joke. I searched Craig's face for a stifled smile, hoping against hope that it was just that.

"You know that every year the army publish the dates for the call-up, in the newspaper," he went on. "Look at the page—you've made it, you're famous! You're in the paper."

"Craig, this is no occasion for humour," I replied.

"If only," said Craig. "You go and check. It's in this morning's *Dominion*."

The army medical was the first brush with my future. The next letter I received confirmed the bad news. I had passed my medical examination, and I was to be in Picton at 11 a.m. on the 5th of January. Not one of my friends had been caught in the ballot. I'd had a secret but forlorn hope that the army medical would show I had flat feet or a missing heartbeat and I'd be turned down.

"You'll enjoy it, Pete!" was the reaction from many, but I wasn't enthused. Summer was just around the corner. Summers were normally about the beach, boats, and killing sandflies—not learning how to kill people.

Fitness would get me through, I decided. It was October, so I had three months to prepare, although I'd later discover that nothing can prepare a carefree teenager for life in the army. 'Carefree' goes out the window. However, my running and bike riding became a daily discipline, and I found myself fitter than I'd ever been. January 5th finally arrived, but the start didn't go well.

"Today you are experiencing a TAB," the corporal who met us at the ferry terminal announced.

It was midday, and the bus journey from Picton to Burnham Military Camp south of Christchurch took about six hours. We'd already had an early start to catch the first ferry.

"You won't know what a TAB is, will you?" the corporal commented with a resigned shrug of his shoulders. "It's a *Typical Army Balls-up!* The bus coming to collect us has only just left Christchurch, so we'll be stuck here for the next five hours," he informed us.

I looked out from the Picton ferry terminal at launches and speed boats, and holiday makers with fishing rods and picnic lunches, laughing and chatting behind sunglasses and under sun hats. The last four years of my life took front place in my memory. I would be swapping swimming togs for 'sandpaper suits,' fishing rods for guns, freedom to make my own calls for obedience to nonsensical commands and demands. *Suck it up,* I thought. I closed my eyes and waited for the bus.

It was 11.30 p.m. when the military police swung open the barriers at the Burnham Military Camp. The six-hour journey from the top of the South Island had sent several of my fellow conscripts to sleep.

"Welcome to your home for the next three months," barked the corporal, bringing most of us back into consciousness. The gate swung shut behind us, and the vehicle slowed to a standstill.

Tumbling down the steps of the military bus we were like a small flock of sheep released from a pen but not knowing what to do next.

"March! Form yourselves into a platoon! Left, right, left, right… You are now in the army. We are off to the quartermaster for your kit. He is not happy, 'cos you are late. So shut up and you should be in the barracks by midnight if you are lucky!"

The dimly lit parade ground and the bright lights of a distant quartermaster store were the most welcoming features of the long night, our first at Burnham Military Camp. The army doesn't allow you to even think. It wasn't our fault we were late. That was clearly now completely irrelevant.

"I want your foot size, shirt size and trouser size when you get to the head of the queue."

I watched in amazement. The first off the rank mumbled, "Size nine boots, medium chest and short legs," and the corporal's team of helpers went into action, skidding our army kit across the polished tabletop that separated us from the crates of army issue. A smell of moth balls mixed with body odour pervaded the large wooden clothing depot. Two pairs of boots hurtled in from nowhere followed by various items of uniform. The corporal may have been just a few years older than us, but he had something sewn onto his sleeve—two stripes that gave him a military-style authority, if nothing else. Clearly, his military training gave him one out of ten for interpersonal skills and ten out of ten for the use of expletives. It also gave him terrific abilities to scream orders and to verbally denigrate his new audience.

I found myself thinking of the war film *Escape from Colditz*. Maybe I could climb the high walls around the Burnham Military Camp tonight and make my escape? Hearing my name being yelled across the depot, I snapped back from the fantasy, scrambled my gear into the army-issued kit bag, and hurried to catch up with twenty-four other young men whose names, histories and hopes I had absolutely no idea about.

The corporal stabbed the air with his finger when we arrived at our sleeping quarters.

"The army calls this *barracks*. It isn't the Hilton Hotel but it does have bunks. Find one and go to sleep." A temporary prefabricated building with twenty-four beds and a gap of about half a metre between each, greeted us. Nobody spoke. We just threw our armfuls of gear onto the first available bed and claimed it for the next thirteen weeks.

I had made a habit of kneeling beside my bed each night and thanking God for everything. The anger and hate that filled the barracks that night had me ducking between the army-issue sheets, shutting my eyes and begging God for forgiveness for being so pathetic 'under fire'. There was no way I could kneel and pray. I had read of an African-American Christian preparing for combat in Vietnam who knelt in a dormitory each night. Boots, books and bottles were hurled at him on the first night as he prayed, but he recounted how by night five he was accepted and became the de facto chaplain to his fellow soldiers—something I did not have the courage to do.

That first night I lay quietly in my army bunk and wondered if I'd arrived in what I could only think of as hell on earth. My mind wandered back to the Marlborough Sounds and the scene that confronted me as I'd disembarked the ferry to wait for the army bus. It wasn't a good start.

Basic training followed—marching, standing on the parade ground, learning how to 'present arms', route marches, cleaning your self-loading rifle again and again. Going to the little theatre and watching films of the New Zealand army fighting the communists in Malaysia, witnessing the horrendous injuries to soldiers and medics bandaging them up, filled each day.

"I can't watch this stuff!" I whispered to a new mate. "Blood and stuff and limbs torn off makes me want to faint." I closed my eyes to protect myself from passing out.

The army demanded and taught that thinking for yourself was a complete *no-no*. Fighting in trenches was 'just obey' stuff. If the platoon commander screamed 'advance', you advanced, which meant that if bullets and bodies were falling all around you, you were to just ignore that and run with guns blazing to wherever the platoon commander pointed. There was some logic in this, which I understood. However, on a sweltering summer's day in a relatively quiet New Zealand army camp, war in the trenches seemed a very distant possibility.

On our first daily two-hour drill parade, a fly landed on my face. We had been standing at attention for what seemed like hours, practicing right turns, left turns, 'falling in', marching in time . . .

The hot summer Canterbury sun mixed with sweat had done its job, and flies, sticky flies, swooped between us looking for a place to land. One chose my face. I flicked it with my hand, which was meant to be by my side.

"Leave the flies alone, Yarrell!" the sergeant bawled at me. "The flies have been here longer than you, so leave them alone!" After that I found that shaking my head sideways quickly was less noticeable and almost as successful at moving the flies on to their next parking place!

They were long days, and if you were lucky enough to faint, as some did, that was a real bonus as you would be carted away to sit in the shade.

Enjoying my privacy was important to me. My heart sank on my first visit to our 'bathroom'. Tucked in behind the rows of barracks was the ablution block. I checked it out. The wooden door swung stiffly on its hinges to reveal a ten-metre-long shower tray made from galvanised iron. At first glance it looked like a tram that had its wheels and seats removed daily—narrow and confined. At every metre on the left side wall was a shower head, and a crude trough that was the drain for the water ran down the right side. Welcome to life in the *raw*!

But it got worse.

The toilets were in a long room. A lengthy timber contraption like a long, low workbench confronted me. An artisan in the army workshops had shaped, every metre or so, bottom-sized seat holes in the timber top. *A clever army 'go fast and go well' plan*, I thought. When busy, the toilet resembled a crowded bus shelter at rush hour. A row of recruits not waiting for a bus, sitting cheek to cheek doing their stuff.

Even the thought of using the toilet in the presence of others was beyond my abilities. I found that by eating meals in the 'mess' quickly I could race off to the toilet as others ate, and mostly (after I learned to time it right) gain two fast minutes to myself.

Have we really got three months of this? I pondered.

The basic training had some lighter moments. The West Melton rifle range was a welcome change from the camp. A couple of hundred infantry soldiers belted out hundreds of rounds of ammunition at targets. This was interspersed with some light-hearted bayonet practice. We had to run twenty-five metres, then plunge our bayonets into a swinging look-alike German soldier dangling from a rope. We were trained to do it by numbers, so we yelled, "one, two, three" as we twisted the bayonet inside the 'stomach' of the straw body.

My mind boggled thinking of doing this in real life combat. The thought of clipping my bayonet onto my rifle, racing forward through some murky Vietnamese swamp, and 'running it through' the stomach of a Viet Cong soldier would have unexpected results. The Viet Cong soldier would be dead, and at the sight of the blood and mess, I would faint beside his fallen body. Swooping upon the two of us, a gravedigger from the New Zealand Army graves department (in civvy life probably a council gardener trained in planting trees) would slap us into a couple of coffins, and just before being lowered into a shallow grave I would be belting the side of my coffin screaming, "I only fainted! Let me out!"

In the midst of the action at the rifle range, a field ambulance occasionally rumbled up and parked behind the line of infantry riflemen as we did our target shooting practice. An army dentist would pull out a field dental chair and a bag of dental paraphernalia, don a white mask, and in a backdrop of machine guns and rifles cracking away, examine our teeth. It was a curious sight. Windblown dust and dirt would soon turn his mask a light grey. Somewhat comforting though, I could imagine a telegram leaving a Saigon post office going from army HQ to my next of kin: *Pete was killed in action today we are sorry to say, but according to his dental records he had no decay in his excellent teeth.*

Toward the end of our six-week basic training in military warfare, my mate Tony brought some unexpected news. "I heard that the army have a need for more officers," he told me. "Tomorrow if we go to the officers' training course selection panel meeting, we may be chosen to go to a special training unit to see if we are officer material."

That sounded like a no-brainer.

"Oh, and by the way, you have to have a degree or be doing one at university." Tony added.

"I only passed school certificate, not university entrance, Tony. But let's see. They may be desperate!" I replied.

The course officer explained to his thirty interested-to-be-officers why the army was needing more. "The war in Vietnam is heating up," he said. "In war the second lieutenant is the most expendable rank we have. As an infantry officer you will lead your platoon into battle, on the ground, running, leading and fighting on the front lines. You have to be an example, a leader of men, courageous, obeying your commanding officer without question. In the Second World War, for every thousand platoon leader second lieutenants, about seven hundred were either killed or severely wounded, whereas for the soldiers they commanded, only two hundred and fifty in every thousand were killed or wounded."

The slightly overweight and under-height interviewing officer with the rank of Major addressed us and waited to see how many of us would fall at the first hurdle and return to our barracks, content with no rank but a better chance of living past age twenty-two.

A dozen or so pushed their chairs back and got up and left the room.

Tony gave me a wink and whispered to me, "We've got nothing to lose except our lives! Let's give it a go. We may fail the course anyway!" Tony had a bright faith and a sense of humour. He added a lot to army life for me, and between us we turned most situations into jokes.

We were culled from our fellow foot soldiers, and our days were now spent in leadership training and testing to see if we were suitable officer material. It was fascinating. The trainers played mind games with us hoping to see us crack under pressure. We had camps where we would be attacked at night with blank rounds fired, and had to plan evacuations and counter attacks. Some of us trainee officers were transferred to the army base at Waiouru. We got to shoot old tanks at the range with recoil-less 25lb anti-tank guns. They created so much percussion pressure that blood would flash across our eyes. We were transferred to other military camps around New Zealand, and life became more varied and almost enjoyable.

On graduation we were saluted and given our second lieutenant commission. The document not only told us that the Queen had commissioned us, she had also signed it to prove it!

We couldn't believe we were in the same army! Where we once marched, we now drove in Land Rovers. Where we once queued in line for meals, we now sat at tables covered in white starched tablecloths. Where we once ate the one option available, we now chose from menus. Where we were once ignored and required to salute officers, we were now the officers that others saluted. Where we obeyed commands without question, we now made the commands and asked the questions. I even had my own toilet off my room!

Of course, accompanying all of this lay the responsibilities of leadership that in a theatre of war were demanding and crucial.

At the back of our minds we remembered the fatality rate amongst junior officers of our rank was very high. Accordingly, we couldn't help but wonder if the commanding officers above us made life comfortable for us purposely as they figured we wouldn't be around for too long to enjoy it!

The army I joined was quite different from the army I left. In even better news, two weeks before we were about to start serious combat training to prepare for Vietnam, the government decided to run down its commitment to the Vietnam War and decided territorial soldiers wouldn't be sent.

MY THOUGHTS

I figured that my Coach planned my army experience. Self-discipline was a low-level flyer in my life, and the New Zealand army identified this flaw and exposed it. I sometimes doubted on face value, the wisdom of my Coach, but in hindsight realised He was doing a brilliant job. It was all preparation for the mountain stages ahead.

STAGE 6

My first break, and some down-hill runs

After my stint in the army I went back to civilian work.

My twelve-months of overseas work experience had widened my world view. The army taught me a lot about human nature, discipline and resilience, as well as the cost of the loss of freedom to be yourself. As a television reporter I had learned the basics of writing and reporting and being relevant. My first after-school job, working as a clerk in an insurance office, 8.30 a.m. to 5 p.m., had shown office politics and time-filling to be a waste of life.

I needed challenge and competition and excitement. AMP Insurance advertised for sales representatives. No sales meant no money. *Hard work. Self-discipline. Make it or break it.* That is me! I decided.

My training course in selling and product knowledge was not comprehensive. "This is a rate book," Bill said, dropping in front of me a dark blue plastic handbook. "Now just find a person who needs insurance, make an appointment, ask their age and how much cover they want, look in the right-hand column and that will tell you the premium, and sign them up!"

I was given some more sketchy basics.

"Just explain, Peter, that if your client wants a policy, it is very simple. Help them fill out a *proposal* covering all the medical questions and details. Then ask them to sign it and pay you the first month's premium. Congratulate yourself on the way home because you have made a sale. If your new client should die, their next of kin collects the sum insured while you have earned your commission, and everyone is happy."

I did expect a little more training.

"That is all the training you need," Bill assured me. "Just learn from your mistakes, and ask me if you get stuck. I am always here for you."

Bill lit his third cigarette. His office had no open windows, no air conditioning, and the door was shut.

"Yes Bill." I tried to cover my mouth with my sleeve, a short-fix filter.

"Bill, is it that easy?" The thought of trying to convince my friends, all like me, unmarried and carefree, took my mind back to the advice my previous manager had given me. "So you want me to sell insurance to people who don't want it…?"

It suddenly sounded prophetic and worrying.

Bill passed me a small booklet. "Here, read this. It is called a *sales track*," he said. "If you follow this, sales will follow you."

My first appointment was sticky. My friend and his new wife needed a policy, but I felt I could be misunderstood, that it would seem I was trading on my friendship to make a sale. I only wanted them to buy if they saw their need, not because we were mates. I suggested they think about it, and said we could meet again in a week or so. I dared not ask them to fill out a proposal form. *Too high-pressure*, I thought.

After one week of calling people, mainly friends, and explaining the advantages of owning an insurance policy, I had nothing to show for my efforts.

"How many sales, Pete, for your first week?" Bill asked me on Friday afternoon.

"I've had a lot of face-to-face interviews," I replied. "However, I need confidence to take it further and fill out a proposal and get a signature. I hate high pressure selling, and because they are friends, well . . . it is just so hard."

"In selling, you have to take consent for granted," Bill explained. "Remember what I taught you. What do those letters stand for in the sales track book I gave you: R-D-R-M-C?"

I remembered that. "Um . . . Relax, Disturb, Relieve, Motivate, Close," I responded.

Bill looked at me and said nothing. Blowing smoke rings gave him a moment to consider the advice he wanted to give me.

"What bits of that do you think you do well, and what do you struggle with?" The smoke hung in the stale air.

"I think I am quite good on everything," I replied. "It is a great track to follow. I just fall at the last hurdle. Everyone likes the idea and they seem very motivated, but when I ask if they want to buy, they all say they will think about it. I get stuck right there."

"We haven't talked about body language have we?" Bill said, introducing a new subject. To my amazement, Bill yawned the biggest yawn I had ever seen and looked away from me.

I had never heard of body language.

"Did you notice me yawn?" Bill continued. "What does that tell you?"

"You are bored, you need sleep and are disinterested, I am not conveying my thoughts clearly, or I am annoying you," I replied.

"Okay, let's try this." Bill leaned towards me, smiled, and nodded. His arms relaxed and he looked me in the eye. "Now how do you feel?"

"Wow! You are attentive, interested, keen to engage me and trust me," I replied.

"Exactly," Bill explained. "You have to closely watch a client's body language and listen carefully to their questions. Their 'hot button' will vary from client to client. Some are concerned with security for their family. Others are worried about a business debt, some about a house mortgage, and others about their health. Talk to them just about that. You will hit their hot button. To close the sale, get out a proposal form and ask just one question," Bill continued. "You have to be certain that you have read their intentions correctly."

"What is that question?" I asked.

"Say, 'I have explained the policy to you as best I can. You need to be healthy enough and your occupation safe enough to have a policy. I can ask you all the questions now. Would you like me to do that?'"

Bill made it sound so easy. "Yes, I understand," I replied.

"The sales track is so important," Bill went on. "No one will do anything in life unless they see the need. If you don't disturb your client with strong reasons for buying, you are wasting your time trying to close the deal."

"Isn't that a bit coercive?" I asked.

"It is called taking consent for granted," he replied. "Whatever you want to buy, whether a pair of shoes, a new shirt or a TV, you look to the salesperson—if you trust them—to help you make the decision. If you are a genuine buyer, then the sale happens. You will find most clients really want to buy if you are motivated to genuinely help them. You will advise them to not buy insurance if there isn't a case for it. You enter into their world *wearing their shoes* and you are doing them a favour by helping them to make the decision."

My thirty-minute conversation with Bill that day was life changing. It sat beside my faith like a close brother. *Treat and care for people as you want them to treat and care for you.* It summed up my thoughts and linked perfectly to my new sales role.

The next week, I had five proposals to hand in to my sales manager and five clients who were delighted to have a policy in place.

I was twenty-one, and it was the end of my second week of working for AMP as an insurance agent. I could hardly sleep with the excitement and fulfilment I felt. Everyone had wanted me to complete the proposals on the spot. When I handed in my week's work each Friday, Bill would offer to buy me lunch. Clients became friends, and the crossflow of ideas between us stimulated conversations that often would go beyond insurance, money, and estate planning. Not only could I afford my car running expenses; soon I would be able to afford a more suitable car.

Selling insurance gradually became easier. Friends liked the idea that their bank loan or hire purchase loan would be repaid, or if they died, money would be left for their families. I learned to recognise body language and listened carefully to the responses to my questions.

My sales rewarded me with recognition in my team and within the company. Many weeks I won *Sales of the Week* competitions and soon became the proud owner of my very own typewriter. I could now type my own letters and reports.

Life was more than just about selling insurance. My sister Ruth played netball. Her team captain, Jill Sunderland, became a close friend. I would watch her team some Saturday mornings. Ruth spoke highly of Jill, and before long she became a regular visitor to our family. What was even more impressive was that her father let her drive the family Holden!

The Saturday games became more interesting when Ruth invited Jill to join her on our annual bible class ski trip. Jill's memory of our first connection is at the Stratford Mountain House at Mt Taranaki. We had skied all day and I had a headache. In her caring way, Jilly had packed a mini chemist shop before leaving home, and dispensed aspirin every couple of hours to me. *A cunning plan,* I thought. Four years later we were married!

Those four years allowed us to save every dollar we could. Jilly lived with her parents, and I lived with mine. Minimal board costs allowed us to save a good deposit for a new home. Returning from our honeymoon, we could hardly wait to move into our new house. Today, as I write, Jilly and I have been married for fifty-three years.

MY THOUGHTS

Failure often precedes success. When I realised that a great product would never sell itself, I became a very quick learner of sales progressions. My chosen career promised me an exceptional opportunity to learn relational skills. It also put me in front of clients with diverse needs and personalities. Every new client would become a friend and would teach me listening skills and at the same time introduce me to world views I needed to understand. Jilly added her strengths to mine on our wedding day and together we quickly learned to support each other in preparation for the adventures ahead.

STAGE 7

A crash in the peloton

I made it a practice to door-knock any home that had nappies (diapers) hanging on a washing line. My sales manager, Bill, had told me that nappies were a 'calling card' for any hard-working insurance adviser. He told me that nappies meant babies, babies meant young families, and young families meant a need for life insurance protection.

After a lunchtime appointment, I was driving home on a country road when I noticed nappies.

Ah, a calling card, I thought.

I felt uneasy knocking on doors. To me it was a sort of cheap door-to-door-salesman approach. But the nappies, flapping on a long wire beside the weather-beaten farm cottage seemed to be waving at me, inviting me in.

"Hello! Mum's inside." Young children jumping their bikes over hay bales gave me a friendly welcome. It was a good feeling. *A promising start*, I thought.

The potholed gravel driveway led me to the wide-open back door of the cottage where various mud-covered gumboots had been kicked off at all angles.

"Mum's inside; just go in," the eldest child invited me.

"No, I can't do that, but can you pop in and tell your mum that she has a visitor?"

I hated these moments as I waited for 'mum' to appear.

The cooking smells drifting out of the cottage told me she was busy. In my mind I had already decided I would get a short "No, thanks."

"Hi, I am Peter, and I wondered if you could give me a few moments," I said when she appeared. It was not the most sophisticated approach. "I hope you don't mind, but I noticed nappies on your washing line, and this suggests you have recently had a baby. I thought you may want to chat about life insurance."

To my surprise, Jane introduced herself to me and replied, "I said to my husband yesterday that we should have life insurance, and look! You arrive on our doorstep! Amazing. Sam is home late most afternoons after milking, so why don't you come back next week and tell us about it?"

It turned out that Sam and Jane had four children, and an appointment was made.

The next week we spent an hour chatting through the family's needs, and I suggested some solutions. Their three older children joined us and sat around the kitchen table listening to our conversation. For a while, they all drank some beer from small glasses, then went back to riding their bikes outside in the farmyard. I was staggered that the children drank beer, and I asked Sam about it.

"I used to let them drink from my glass," he said, "but that was totally unacceptable. I took control and said if they wanted to drink beer they had to drink out of their own glasses."

I wasn't sure if Sam was joking, but Jane quickly added that they were only allowed a few sips.

I never dreamed that six months later I would be sitting in the cottage once again, only this time, Sam was not there. Jane was crying as I explained how the death proceeds would be paid out following the car crash that had just killed her husband.

I couldn't attend Sam's funeral but found out he was killed by a drunk driver who had lost control of a Coca-Cola truck he had stolen from outside the same pub where Sam was drinking that night.

In my heart of hearts I had to answer a big question that day. I had become good friends with Sam and Jane prior to his death. The insurance money would give Jane a future without money worries, and a new home to live in, but I thought that I could have done much more.

Death comes with more questions than answers. Jane would be asking *What if, what if, what if?* I wondered if I had the right to address issues and life choices with my clients beyond my brief of arranging their insurances. I was confident that Sam and I had a good relationship. Perhaps I could have talked more seriously about the dangers of alcohol abuse when I saw his young children drinking beer. They may not have listened or taken my advice, but that didn't absolve me from the responsibility of at least raising the topic.

Jane told me that Sam, on his drive home from the hotel that night, was also impaired by the alcohol he had consumed. Had he not been, he might have had quicker reactions and been able to swerve to avoid the truck that had crossed the centre line and killed him.

Sam's children often asked Jane, "Where is Daddy now? Was he just sleeping for a while?" Jane would tell them that he was 'with the angels'. It was a child's question, and understandably, that answer was the best she could give.

Jane confided in me that Sam's sudden death left her feeling confused, angry, and lonely. Clearly a floodlight was now searching her deepest thoughts. *Is life random? Are some people lucky, whilst others dreadfully unlucky?*

We chatted through the alternatives. I told Jane I believed that life isn't random, and that there is a purpose and plan behind everything. "There are many questions that don't have immediate answers," I said, but I felt lightweight and unconvincing. I had nothing within me to show Jane why I believed this. There was only one thing I was sure about, but at the time didn't want to raise it. Sam had played with fire when he went drinking and driving. He paid a huge penalty, now Jane and her family had to live with its consequences, and there were no simple answers.

I tried as best I could to explain to Jane that the gift of life isn't an accident, but I didn't know where to go to from there. The questions that were asked of me all those years ago on the hop farm in England were being asked again but from a different angle and in response to a different need.

This was the first time in my life that I had to stare at the finality and pain of death at close quarters. My heart ached for Jane and her four children. I knew that they looked at me with appreciation for the insurance payout, however that seemed superficial in that moment. I could see that Jane was looking to me for words of comfort and hope, and I struggled to give them.

MY THOUGHTS

The tour took a big turn. A fellow rider, a new friend, left me unexpectedly. It asked questions of my ride. Disturbed now, I began to think. There was no doubt, from the evidence apparent on the tour so far, that an unseen hand was busy at work in me and around me. Jane needed a relationship with my Coach too, and it would help her enormously, but I was completely out of my depth as to how I could introduce her to Him. I was immersed twenty-four hours a day in sales, sport, success, and a family of my own, but this was a curve ball from left field. I had bumped into the coalface of the reason for our very existence, and how I interpreted the tragedy of untimely death suddenly mattered. Sam's death had not only changed the course of his family's life, it was about to change ours too.

STAGE 8

Which route?

My hunting-ground for insurance clients took me onto the farms of Manawatu, a region in the lower North Island of New Zealand where good, hard-working dairy people shook hands, and that meant business. Every new client interview challenged me to talk beyond insurance and to raise the life and death issues that had arisen from Sam's death.

I could not escape my thoughts as I drove home from some of those appointments. On one day, a north-west storm was accompanied by horizontal rain that came in sheets for a few minutes then disappeared into patches of sunlight.

You have everything you ever wished for materially, and you are just twenty-seven, a voice in my head said.

Yes, true, I answered myself. *You have a caring and good wife, two children, a yacht in the Marlborough Sounds, a beautiful car, scores of insurance clients, a beachfront house, a very good income, and yet you know deep down you are not satisfied. You know there is something more to life.* This was the recurring theme in my mind.

I argued with my troubling thoughts. Yes, the yacht could be bigger, the Jaguar newer and my income even higher, but I was unsure if that would spin my wheels any faster.

The thought came to me, *You have a tail wind and a gentle down-slope, plus a fast bike. You have got it made.*

Suddenly, I felt very content. But it only lasted a few moments, because a very strange thing happened. For the first time in my life, my whispering Coach who had watched over me since I was fifteen and had intervened on many occasions without me even asking, suddenly turned up the volume. It was very exciting but incredibly scary. The non-coercive soft voice I heard that day spoke with care and love.

"Yes, Peter. All is well right now," He said. "On your *Tour of Life*, however, if you look carefully, you will see a tight sweeping bend ahead that you need to slow down for. When you round it, you will be given an option. The road splits in two. The left-hand fork will appeal, and it's fast and fun. But it isn't what it seems. The right-hand fork will take you to places beyond anything you can imagine, but it demands more than you can give. I will be with you regardless of your choice. You have a free will and I'm not going to trample on that. From now on there will be two voices on your race radio. Only you can decide which one to follow."

I could see the bend ahead and touched my brakes. It was a pleasant place to stop, and it bought me time.

The Coach needed to answer some very important questions. I could see my future and it seemed to have a golden glow. Sure enough, I'd only stopped for a few seconds, but I could smell the leather in a brand-new Jaguar; I could see my name published in lights for achieving sales bigger than ever; I could feel pleasures and satisfaction abounding; I could even hear a voice in my head making me think that my Coach wasn't really fussed about which fork in the road I selected.

Snapping back into the present, I parked the Jag in the garage and turned off the headlights, but sat for a few moments. I found myself listing a number of questions that I needed to ask my Coach. They were perfectly fair and reasonable.

He spoke again. "Peter, the left fork is by far the most popular. It will involve no change for you in the short term. You will want for nothing." I detected an inference in the Coach's voice around the words short-term. But I didn't ask Him to explain. Something else was on my mind.

"And the right fork?" I asked. "You said it would ask of me more than I could give."

"I can't tell you too much," my Coach replied, "but the right fork will cause you to depend upon me for survival, and that is pretty unnatural."

Unnatural? I thought. I had learned to depend entirely upon myself for our income, and the worry of misunderstanding my Coach and recklessly diving into something that left our family out in the cold was something I couldn't contemplate. Was He asking me to leave the security of my work?

"Okay," I responded. "If this is You talking to me, just show me the destination—like, show me where we will end up if we take the right fork. After all, it isn't just me involved here. Jilly and the children have to buy in as well."

"No deal!" the voice in my head responded.

"Now come on," I retorted. "At least give me a route map. Just let me get prepared … Are there mountains and valleys or rivers to cross? Are there giants? Are there dangers, or ill health? Will we be safe? Will Jilly and our children, Simon and Juliet, come with me? And the big question … who will pay the bills?"

The option ahead of me was quite simple. Should we go left, with all the security that road would provide, or should we turn right, with seemingly no security, no destination revealed, and no understanding of the dangers along the way?

Down the left-hand fork was a brilliant, safe road. I could see everything as it stretched into the distance: influence, sales with higher commissions, new friends, security, travel, luxury yachts. The images and satisfaction in my head seemed to make it a no-brainer. I loved seeing my name as *Salesman of the Week* at my insurance office. What a future! However, there were a few not-so-good distractions that could lead me down paths I did not want to travel; distractions that I wondered if I had the power to resist…

It was November 1970. The new year was just two months away. There was no real option.

Steady as she goes, Pete, I said to myself, as I left my parked car in the garage. *Forget it. Christmas is coming and then a big year ahead. Crowd out these thoughts.*

"Yes," I concluded, "we will take the left fork."

Christmas did come, and 1970 had brought success upon success in the sales world. Family, snow-skiing, sailing and golf filled in my time between sales.

I dared to think of my 'fork option' vision occasionally. If fulfilment from asset accumulation was my end goal, that had lost all its appeal. However, my desire to see my name in lights and the fun and fulfilment from making sales was still thick in my veins, and it made it easy to justify the left fork in the road.

But the offer of the right-hand roadway sat in the back of my head and wouldn't go away. As a strong rider in a peloton chooses the moment to make his or her ride off the front (called a break), so I had a sense that I needed to build up enough strength mentally, physically and spiritually to break away from the security of everything I had grown to depend upon over the previous six years.

Curiously, the next twelve months were not what I'd expected. Yes, sales had never been better. Commissions and client numbers increased. However, I was locked up in a battle in my conscience, so I tried to just work harder and socialize more, hoping my conscience would stop bothering me. I couldn't put out of my mind Sam's death and the sudden and tragic end to his life. I found that I became more and more aware of my growing attraction to materialism and all that went with it.

My Coach turned up the volume a notch. He simply wouldn't give up on me. I could see myself being dropped from the peloton if I didn't make a decision quickly.

The year was slipping by, and with no logical reason I began to have an empty and lonely feeling that I couldn't shake. I had turned my back on my Coach, but my Coach hadn't turned His back on me. I needed to go back into negotiation with Him.

"What's next," I asked. "Do we pack up, sell up, and head to a theological college in Auckland? Oh and how do we pay the bills, and where do we live, and will Jilly agree?"

My Coach responded. "Come on, Pete. Take the first steps on the right-hand path and live the dream." The Coach was starting to yell at me, and I remembered the times I had ignored His voice and paid with the consequences.

"Yes, but what happens when my commission cheques are almost zero? How do I pay the bills?" I argued. Riding the right-hand road dream could well turn into a nightmare. If I took the first pedal strokes on the right-hand road, I knew deep down there would be no U-turns.

"Just give me the assurance that we will have a house to live in, an income to live on, and a great destination. If so, I am pushing 'Go' for the right-hand fork," I bargained with my Coach.

But I got no comfort from Him.

"Give me one more year, just one extra year and then I will have money saved and we will be financially secure for a year or two."

Now that is logical, I thought. *How about that?*

"Last year was one more year, Peter," I was reminded.

For no human reason, in the middle of this storm of negative and worrying thoughts, a sense of peace settled in my heart. With my hands on my handlebars, I leaned to the right, slowed a little, and gently steered onto the right-hand fork.

I knew I could turn back if Jilly didn't think she could join me on the adventure. I felt that was the only condition for turning back the Coach would grant me. A part of me hoped for that, knowing it would give me a justifiable reason to return and ride the left fork and live the life of security and predictability I really enjoyed.

I tried to give Jilly the downside and my doubts, as well as the upside. I struggled with the upside knowing that truthfully, I was unsure of it myself, but Jilly amazed me. "Peter, if that is what you think we should do then we will do it," she said when I mentioned the idea of going to theological college. I seriously wondered if I trusted myself, but it didn't matter. Jilly had all the trust we needed.

I had put all my bets on my Coach, but still I woke some nights tossing and turning and wondering if my conversations with my Coach were just imagined.

Unsure of our next steps, I applied to a theological college in Auckland and was accepted to do a three-year course in preparation for becoming a minister. We had four months to sell up and pack down. Austerity and challenges were afoot. I dared not tell my parents until January, once we'd secured an Auckland house to live in. By then we were past the point of no return.

MY THOUGHTS

My Coach showed patience with me but never quite let me climb off my bike. Now the tour would begin in earnest. The smell of the rich leather in the Jaguar was about to be swapped for the smell of an over-worked engine in the second-hand Mini we crammed the family into on our trip to Auckland. The sense of the journey into the unknown came with the excitement of anticipation and somehow suppressed any feelings of the impending austerity we were about to have to get used to. We were onto the mountain stages now, and the road ahead was steep and at times completely out of our comfort zones. The good news? We would have occasional glimpses of the Coach when He needed to pump up our tyres and oil the chain. He just seemed to keep saying to me, "Be strong and courageous."

STAGE 9

Road works. Slow down!

Mr Collins, my sales manager at the insurance company, accepted my resignation with regret.

"Three years of theological training?" Mr Collins looked curious. "Are you sure?"

He respected me enough not to discourage me, and said he would transfer my insurance agency to Auckland if I could find time to sell and study at the same time. I guessed he fully expected that within three months I would return to his team, licking my wounds.

Studying theology turned out to be everything I had hoped it wouldn't be. Professional religion seemed to be completely disconnected from the reality of life in the business sector, out on the streets I had walked for the past six years. Some of my fellow students seemed to me to have every ounce of spirit choked out of them—if it was ever there in the first place. I was disappointed, and by the end of the first term I began to understand why. I had expected energy, vitality, wisdom, and genuine belief. I found the opposite—unbelief, and liberal thinking that seemed to me to cause doubts and academic smugness. I looked for love and humour, creativity and truth, but I found just theories. The whole environment was out of touch with the world I had lived in since I had left school.

So, I made a plan! Taking courage in both hands I knocked on the solid timber door of the principal's office.

"Yes, Mr Yarrell?" The principal, a Doctor of Theology, seemed to want to ignore me—he just kept reading a journal on his otherwise paper-free desktop and made no eye contact. His gloomy office summed up my feelings.

"I just don't get Greek," I said, "and I am finding that this college isn't quite what I'd expected."

Without looking up, he reached across to the left of his carved oak desk, opened a drawer and took out a pad of paper, and wrote *Delete Yarrell Greek* on it.

I thought back to my sales manager at AMP and remembered the way he treated me when I dropped into the sales office. He would tell his secretary to hold all calls and visitors, to make me a coffee and find some cake, then he would shut the office door to give me his undivided attention for as long as I needed it. Those days were long gone.

"Anything else?" the principal kept his eyes on the journal he was reading.

"I don't think so," I replied.

I turned and exited the door I had just come through and went back to my study shaking my head. *What on earth am I doing here?* I asked myself.

My thoughts returned to the fork in the road and the left-hand turn back into my old reality and prosperity.

However my Coach had a Plan B.

Capernwray, named after a castle in Northern England, was an international study and live-the-dream college set on a large Howick seaside property. It turned out a two-roomed cottage was vacant. This was made available to us for three months. What a difference! The lecturers were fun, faith-filled, real people who obviously lived what they believed.

One of the lecturers, Charles Price from England, arrived at the same time we did. Charles' communication skills, his obvious dynamic relationship with the Coach and his sense of humour kept us riveted.

In later years, Charles was appointed to lead The People's Church in Toronto, and became a household name across Canada with a TV programme titled *Living Truth*. But for us in the meantime, a small class of students, he was a Coach-send.

In Auckland, school fees plus living expenses needed to be met, but my insurance sales had stalled completely, and our savings had disappeared like overnight snow on a hot morning. I had tried half-heartedly to make a few sales, without success. I knew no one, and Auckland people seemed different from my clients and friends down south. I just didn't connect with them.

I'd never owed anyone money and paying bills on time was never a problem. Until now.

"Ask and it shall be given unto you," I spoke in prayer, along with a quote from the Lord's Prayer: "Give us this day our daily bread." Quickly I added, "Oh yes, and by the way, Lord, this is urgent!" I thought that the Coach may stir up a friend who would pop a couple of thousand dollars into my bank mysteriously. After all, He had got me into this, I mused.

No mysterious money in my bank account turned up. However, my prayer made me think that I should take the afternoon off school and do some door-knocking in a nearby street.

I found a street near the school where new houses were being constructed. I felt so alone and unsure of myself, but I was sure of one thing—sitting in the car feeling anxious was not going to get me anywhere. It would only lead to self-pity.

Grasping courage with both hands, I locked the driver's door of the Mini and crossed the roadway to the entrance of the new subdivision. I noticed a builder struggling with a long ladder as he was lifting it off his roof rack.

"Afternoon," I greeted him. "Can I give you a hand?" I felt anxious and self-conscious and was glad he accepted my offer. I ran through in my mind words that I could use.

"My name is Yarrell, Peter Yarrell, and I wondered if you are in need of any advice on insurance?" I felt utterly stupid and unprofessional.

The builder put down his ladder and looked at me. A smile spread across his face. "Hi! My name is Robert," he said, shaking my hand. "Amazing! As a matter of fact, I had a call from my bank manager this morning and he said that the bank would lend me the money for the next house if I had $30,000 of life insurance. Come on in and give me some numbers."

Threading my way past cables and fittings left around by electricians and plumbers, I followed Robert into his almost-completed spec house.

Robert waved his hand at the newly-installed kitchen top. "Here, please rest your briefcase on this."

After thirty minutes, I had heard Robert's story. As a 'spec' builder, he hoped each house he built would have a buyer before it was finished and he started on the next one.

"We've had a bit of a hiccup," Robert explained. "This house is all but finished and I have the foundations down for my next. My problem is that I have not sold this one, and my bank won't lend me any money without life insurance. I can't wait too long to get onto my next house, so I need some insurance now."

Over the noise of skill-saws and electric drills I listened to Robert's story and asked questions that would allow me to suggest some answers. I simply couldn't believe this conversation. Robert wanted to sign up for the biggest policy I had ever sold. I wondered for a moment if I could feel the wind of angels' wings hovering overhead.

We signed the proposals, and Robert shook me by the hand. We met as complete strangers and parted an hour later having won each other's confidence and trust. Robert kept his bank manager happy, and his next house project got underway. Within four weeks I received the commission and was able to pay all my outstanding accounts.

I don't remember driving back to Capernwray that day, but I do remember feeling dazed by the afternoon's events. My heart was dancing inside my ribcage, not just because of the sale, but also with the sense of an awesome presence working within.

I opened the kitchen door of our little cottage. "Pete, you are home early." Jilly looked out from behind the small pantry door. "How did you get on?" she asked.

I didn't need to answer the question. Jilly just looked at the smile on my face and shared with me the gratitude in my heart.

MY THOUGHTS

This stage on tour was almost 'give up and call for your support vehicle' territory. The struggles on the first part of the stage made me really question my decision to take this route. If meeting Robert was a coincidence, that was fine. So many threads had been woven together in front of my eyes: the timing of my parking the car and walking across the road just at the moment Robert needed help with the ladder; his need for help presenting a natural introduction; his meeting with his bank manager that morning; his willingness to trust me, not to mention the amount of insurance he needed. Every thread in the tapestry was necessary for that moment to exist. What snapped it out of coincidence territory were my prayers, prayed with a measure of desperation that morning.

STAGE 10

Changing gears

Graduation day was approaching, and I had to start looking past that day and get some direction from the Coach as to where the next stage would take us. He was up to His old tricks again and gave me no road map that could bring me confidence or concrete answers for the family. However, a random journal appeared in the school common room that attracted my attention. I had thirty minutes to spare, so I picked it up, grabbed a glass of water, and skim-read the contents.

Stop, stop, Pete! Read that bit carefully! My brain suddenly felt it needed to go into slow motion.

In the journal were a couple of brief paragraphs about a 'find your purpose for living' story based in a centre called L'Abri in the Swiss mountains, and a review of a book written by the wife of the founder of L'Abri, Mrs Edith Schaeffer. The journal mentioned the name of the book and where it could be bought.

Before I knew it, I was driving my Mini town-wards, glancing anxiously at my watch. I hurried through every traffic light as I ducked and dived between the traffic to reach the bookshop before it closed at 5 p.m. With five minutes to spare, I captured my copy of the book and headed to the Westhaven Marina. I parked the car under the Auckland Harbour Bridge, where I was confident there were no parking meters and no one to disturb my read.

It wasn't since I'd read Louis Zamperini's book *Devil at my Heels* that I'd been so engaged and hungry to think about every word.

Edith Schaeffer's book, *L'Abri,* is the story of the Schaeffer family's journey from the USA to the mountains of Switzerland. Dr Schaeffer and his wife, Edith, called their new home *L'Abri* (The Shelter) and invited guests to join them if they had a desire to find faith or were honestly seeking answers to questions that may help them on their journey. Her book tells fascinating stories of miracles, hard work, frustrations and prayers answered as they opened their home to seekers that arrived on their doorstep.

Every page made my heart leap. Edith's words spoke into my life in a way that few books previously had. It was like putting a battery in a torch.

Our journey, which till then had been like riding in dense fog, now had a shaft of sunlight that not only illuminated the future but explained the purpose of the past. I sensed a tailwind blowing for the first time on the right-hand fork road. The clouds had parted enough to allow us to focus on the road ahead, and my head was buzzing. It was as if we had been flying an aircraft through clouds that part for a second, just long enough for some snow-covered mountains to flash into view then disappear again. I could barely believe it. At last the road ahead gave me a glimpse of the future.

How I would love to open my bible and receive such affirmation for a plan that was formulating in my head, I thought out loud.

My bible sat beside me on the passenger seat of the Mini. I reached across and opened it at random. The page fell open to Micah chapter four, and my eyes landed on the following words: "*Come, let us go up to the mountain of the Lord, to the house of . . . God. He will teach us his ways so that we may walk in his paths*" (v. 2).

I stared at the verse in awe. Time seemed to stand still. I read it again.

What is going on?

I read it yet again.

Now that is amazing, I mused. Edith Schaeffer had read a very similar verse, only from another book of the bible, before moving to Switzerland. I didn't realise those words were repeated in the book of Micah.

I felt like a blind man who had just had his eyes opened. My drive through the evening traffic jam of Auckland back to Capernwray gave me time to contemplate our future.

Jilly and I had a discovered the beautiful Wakatipu region of New Zealand as teenagers. I'd learned to ski on Coronet Peak, and just as the many visitors like us had found, our hearts were captivated. Many describe the area as the Switzerland of the Pacific.

Was our love affair with the South Island paradise of New Zealand, centred around the alpine village of Queenstown, about to begin? Perhaps the Coach was waving a road map under our noses to head south.

MY THOUGHTS

A year had now gone by since I'd leaned into the right-hand corner to ride the right-hand fork. Had the Coach shown His hand at the beginning and told me what was in store, would I have ridden this road? Probably not. Knowing us, He had no option but to hide His plans, or we would have fallen at the first hurdle. Did I need to worry about the next twelve months and the direction the road would take? Yes, but it was different now. I had built a small reservoir of confidence in the Coach.

I felt I'd heard first-hand, straight from the mouth of the Coach, and in so doing I now had a glimpse of where we were heading. This was an amazing stage. I began to realise that the Coach wasn't just limited to speaking over the race radio. It was suddenly more intimate. I sensed there was something big ahead.

STAGE 11

The mountain stages

The Mini could have won a competition for how much we could fit into it and still have room for two adults and two children plus all our worldly belongings, then travel 1500 kilometres. After making the crossing on the Interislander ferry to the South Island, however, we had to make a call. In a unanimous vote, we agreed to sell the Mini and buy a second-hand Land Rover and a caravan to make life a little more bearable.

On arriving in the Wakatipu, we parked the caravan and explored our new surroundings. We looked for some land and door-knocked a few farmhouses, which proved to be a wise plan.

"Yes, I do have some land for sale. Just subdivided it," said one man. Standing on his back porch amongst a pile of muddy, randomly kicked-off gumboots, the farmer was few on words and not welcoming. He waved his arm and pointed toward a sloping hill about five hundred metres to the north and passed me a survey plan that indicated boundaries.

"Have a wander up that hill and see what you think." Without another word he turned and shut the homestead door behind him.

With survey plan in hand, we couldn't believe our eyes. If we read the plan correctly, there were about seventy walnut trees on the ten acres of south-facing land that was for sale. We imagined where the best place would be for a building platform and stood on it envisaging a house, whilst drinking in the view of Lake Hayes.

The next morning I took a deep breath, pushed past the same muddy gumboots that were there the day before, and once again knocked on the homestead's back door. Bill, the landowner, looked surprised to see me.

This time I not only clutched the plans under my arm, but also a sales agreement in case Bill made a decision about our offer on the spot.

With Queenstown just twenty kilometres to the west, Arrowtown a five-minute drive to the north, and a view of Lake Hayes, we had a fabulous site if he'd agree to our offer. I reckoned if my first offer was rejected, I'd have little chance to make a second. He gave me the feeling he wouldn't open his door another time to a young enthusiastic dreamer from the North Island.

"What did you think?" The farmer seemed a little more communicable.

"Well, if we understand the survey plan correctly, we'd like to buy the lower of the two ten acre blocks you have for sale."

A price that we thought fair sat in the forefront of my mind, but I was unsure if it was the right time to suggest a price. I just looked Bill in the eye and waited for him to continue the conversation.

"What are you prepared to pay?" Bill came straight to the point, taking me by surprise.

"Well, could I ask you what you had in mind?" I felt jumpy as I realised that our future and all our plans hung on his reply in the next few brief seconds.

"I'm not going to fence it," he said. "That is your expense, but I do want to sell."

"Yes," I said, and continued to wait. We had done some sums using a wild guesstimate of a build price. Bill just had to say the number we could afford.

"You have got a document there." He pointed to my left hand. "If you do the electric power, the fences, and a water supply, it's yours for —"

Before I could say any more, he mentioned the exact figure Jilly and I had decided on two hours earlier. I left the back door with the sales agreement signed and the numbers agreed to, scarcely able to contain my excitement.

It was lunch time when I parked the Land Rover beside our caravan. With a wide smile and a grateful heart I dropped the signed agreement on the caravan's camp table. Our southern adventure had begun.

I had to cover the downsides with Jilly. Before the first holes could be dug for the fence posts, the boundary lines had to be established, and the farmer was not interested in helping us with that. A water source had to be found by drilling, or by pumping water out of a stream a hundred and fifty metres away, and electricity would have to be trenched in. With four hundred metres of fencing needed, we had weeks of hard work ahead. The post holes needed to be dug every five metres by hand over rolling hills peppered with tree roots and stones. In the hot Central Otago summer weather, it would be exhausting work (not to mention challenging and complicated for an insurance salesman!), but achievable.

We parked our caravan under a walnut tree and dug a long-drop toilet. From that point on, the days began with Jilly and our two-year-old daughter, Juliet, collecting trailer-loads of posts and coils of wire from town, while our four-year-old son, Simon, assisted me as best he could.

With no water on site, late each afternoon Jilly loaded Simon and Juliet into the back of our car and we headed off to the Arrowtown camping ground for hot showers, proper toilets, and dish-washing facilities. The slot-machine washer and dryer proved a challenge for Jilly as she had to find the coins, but it soon became an evening routine. After refillling our twenty-litre jerry cans with water, we headed back to the caravan ready for a recharge of sleep, dinner and rest.

Our building permit arrived in the mail at the end of February 1973. Earlier, we had met our builder, Murray Paterson, at Capernwray. He told us that his building work for overseas missions had finished, and he'd be keen to build our new home. Armed with one small skill-saw and a toolbox, he arrived on site in January 1973, complete with his tent, to begin the building programme. Now Jilly had an 'extra' every night for dinner in the caravan. Life became slightly more complicated—Jilly hadn't been feeling well for a while, and arrived home one day after seeing her doctor with the news that she was once again pregnant!

By late May, the ground was frozen solid.

"Pete, I can't stay upright walking around the hill to the long-drop with all the ice. Even your old golf shoes won't stop me from slipping and sliding. We really can't keep living in the caravan now winter has come," she rightly observed.

Jilly was far more practical than me. I realised I was so focused on the building project, working ten-hour days, that I neglected details to do with the caravan. Progress was slow, but we were getting close to the roofers arriving and the prospect of a 'close-in' in the next two months. Simon and Juliet were happy spending most mornings sliding on the icy floors of the unfinished house, or down the hills on the sledge. Still, moving into a house was imperative.

As we thought about this, I received a call from my sister Wendy.

"It must be freezing there now," she said. "I met a lady, a widow, in Invercargill. She has recently moved to Frankton, just ten minutes from you. Her name is Rua. She has a flat under her house. Even if you don't want to live in her flat, you must go and meet her. She is gorgeous, one of the most amazing people I have ever met. Here is her address."

Treetops turned out to be a renovated old 'crib' (the local word for a small holiday house). We lined up at Rua's front door that cold May day, like a huddling refugee family.

"Darlings!" we were greeted with enthusiasm. "Wendy told me you may come and see me."

Rua bottled up so much love that when she met her many visitors that needed help, like us, she had just the one greeting.

"Of course, you can stay! I just had some long-termers unexpectedly move out and I would love you to have my little flat—providing you think it is big enough."

As we got to know Rua, we began to doubt if there was anyone on the planet that could match her for unconditional love, perception of needs, practical help, and faith. She was the hub for anyone in Queenstown who wanted to share their hopes, their troubles, or their faith—her door was always open to them. Widowed just eighteen months earlier, Rua had been through more heartache and death than we could imagine or bear, yet you would never know. She lived on a surfboard of faith riding a tidal wave of hope, towards a beach called heaven. Rua was beautiful physically, mentally and spiritually. She became Jilly's best friend and the children's adopted grandmother, as well as hostess of a weekly newcomers' group we started together, called *Wednesday's at Rua's*.

She explained her financial approach to life. "I have champagne tastes but I have to live on a beer income," Rua explained with a giggle. Rua's two bedroom apartment captured a stunning view up Lake Wakatipu from Frankton. Edging the lake below were random willow trees, with the mountain peaks behind Queenstown all back-dropped by the snow-topped 2500-metre Walter and Cecil Peaks. By day we worked on our new property, and by night we lived in her cosy apartment.

The months came and went, and by December we were ready to move into our almost-completed house!

For all my struggles with Greek the previous year, we thought a good name for our new property would be *Koinonia*. Translated, this means 'fellowship'. Passionate as we were for community, our vision was far more than that. Simply put, we saw a place where faith and fun, love and belonging, sharing with caring, and the physical, the mental and the spiritual makeup of life worked together in harmony.

Adding to our housewarming, we welcomed into our family our beautiful new baby, Angela. Simon and Juliet helped Jilly with baby duties, and the children readily chatted with all our day-guests as well as those who stayed a few days. With our new dog in tow, they would take visitors on a tour of the ten acres and introduce them to our two horses that my fences kept penned in most of the time.

Many guests shared our dining room table. We were learning lessons continually. Realising we were beginners, we found that living at close quarters with people we had never met before has its pleasures, its pain, and its pressures. Sometimes we had to dig deep to find the grace to overcome our natural reactions. We had many supportive, caring guests, and others we found turning the other cheek and accepting a slap across the face was the wisest (but most humbling) solution for the moment. There were volumes to learn about ourselves, and with every bump in the road we could look back and see that both good times and more difficult times combined to take us forward as well as to change us.

One golden thread carried us along. There was always a solution, always an important lesson to learn. We just had to ask forgiveness when we stuffed up.

There were regular stand-out occasions that extended us and interrupted our normal days. It was Christmas 1975, and our long dining table was elbow-to-elbow with guests enjoying the celebrations. Amidst the children exploring Christmas presents, the conversations and laughter, Jilly had concentrated her efforts, willingly assisted by some of our guests, to produce a Christmas dinner for everyone.

A knock on the door added another couple to the already-packed table. On answering it, we met Jim and Jenny, a couple who had a caravan parked in nearby Cromwell and had been encouraged by mutual friends to come and visit.

It was later that afternoon, when we said goodbye to Jim and Jenny that I noticed that Jim, who was in his seventies, I guessed, looked quite unwell.

Later that week, I received a phone call.

"Hi Peter, Jenny here." Over the phone, her voice was soft and slow. I tried to remember how Jenny fitted into my existing world, but my mind was slightly overcrowded with Christmas guests.

Jenny refreshed my memory. "Jim and I had Christmas dinner with you on Thursday," she said. "We have the caravan at the Cromwell Motor Camp."

"Yes, yes, of course," I replied. "How is everything?"

"Peter, this is a strange request, but I really need you to help me," Jenny replied. "About half an hour ago, Jim died. He was resting on the narrow bunk in our pop-top caravan and just slipped away. I knew he was weak and very sick, but it has really hit me."

I waited for Jenny to continue. "Driving back from Lake Hayes on Christmas day with you, we felt that if anything happened to Jim . . ." her voice trailed off.

"Yes?" I waited.

"Well, Jim and I discussed in the car, that if he died, we would like you to come down to our caravan and sort things out. Can you come immediately?"

Cromwell was one hour's drive on the busy road that runs through the Kawarau Gorge. I tucked my bible into the car in case I needed words of comfort, then tried to think of what I would say to Jenny in her grief.

I had never been into the Cromwell camping ground before and was surprised by the number of holidaymakers, but on seeing a police car parked close to the pop-up roof caravan, I guessed word had got around camp of the death.

Jenny ran to my car and took my hand. I was grateful to her for this as I was struggling to remember her face.

"Thank you so much for coming, Peter. I had to stop the police from organising a funeral director to take Jim away. I told them you were on the way and everything would be good."

I was expecting Jenny to ask me to pray and was ready to read a psalm to comfort her. Realising Jenny was unfamiliar with Cromwell, I expected her to ask for advice on a local minister or church to contact.

I had forgotten how little room there is in a pop-top caravan. Jim had been placed on his back on the floor between the two parallel beds. Jenny squeezed her feet beside Jim's body and sat on the left-hand bed. I was able to squeeze in beside her, tucking my feet under Jim's legs as Jenny spoke. "Peter, we believe that you are going to bring Jim back to life. After the Christmas dinner last week, Jim had a strong thought. We had taken him off the pills that he needed to keep him alive, but we did so knowing that him coming back to life would be a statement to the world that God can still raise people from the dead." Jenny took a breath.

"So, Jenny, you are expecting Jim right now to come back to life?" I wanted to make sure I had heard correctly.

"Yes," she replied. "Jim and I are looking to you to do this for us now. We knew you would come. I told my sister in Palmerston North that you were on the way down from Arrowtown, and I also told the police that they could not take Jim away as he is going to come back to life. Our church is believing that this will be a sign to New Zealand that through Jim coming back to life, God will be honoured in a very special way." Jenny choked back tears.

I glanced down at Jim's ashen face. Thoughts ran through my mind so quickly. I'd had no idea what I was being called to do when I'd left Lake Hayes just an hour earlier.

Dear God, I thought. *Do I respond by anointing Jim's head with oil? Do I pray for him to come back to life? Do I breathe oxygen into his mouth? Do I take his hand and lift him up? Do I have the necessary faith or power of God within me to bring a person back from the dead? Should I even try? Do I have the inspiration and wisdom to guide Jenny to simply accept Jim's death?*

I popped my arm around Jenny's shoulder and prayed, and a peaceful stillness settled.

"Dear God, if it is your plan to bring Jim back to live in his body, we simply ask you to do this now."

I took a moment, then carried on. "As you have released Jim from his sick body, we can also ask you not to bring him back. We both know that he loves you, and we don't want to be so selfish as to pray he be brought back to us if that is our plan and not yours…"

Jenny interrupted my prayers.

I glanced down at Jim's lifeless body, wondering if Jenny had seen him move.

"Peter, Peter! I understand Jim is with God. Why would I want him back in his sick body?"

I was amazed at Jenny's complete change of heart.

"Why would we want Jim to be back in his sick body when he is now released from it? I get it! … I get it…" she said. "He is truly healed!"

We sat together in silence for a minute. Jenny was plainly lost in her thoughts. Eventually she turned to me and whispered, "The police can take control now."

I arrived back at Lake Hayes to a very buzzy *Koinonia*. An elderly Australian Baptist minister had just arrived to stay for a few days. I needed someone to share my story with, and he listened intently.

"You did that right, Pete," he assured me. "I have, on one occasion, been asked to pray to bring a parishioner back to life. You see, no one really dies," the minister continued. "Just the body dies. Why would the spirit want to come back to live in a worn out or sick body?"

MY THOUGHTS

This stage started with hard-out training, but we discovered unexpected help, energy and power in the peloton when we were riding alongside Rua. The guests, their life stories, and the accompanying pressures they brought into the family took us beyond our expectations, however. Life is dynamic and we were experiencing that in the fast lane. When I prayed about Jim, Jenny quickly changed her mind. It was like she'd had a 'Spirit of God lightning bolt' hit her. The person I was as I stepped into her caravan was entirely different to the person I was when I stepped out. I found myself questioning a few things about their decisions to stop taking medication, but I wasn't asked to comment on this. I hoped that I hadn't let them, or God, down. The consoling and comforting words of the Australian Baptist minister settled any anxiety I was feeling.

STAGE 12

Team tactics

For ten years we laughed, loved and learned at *Koinonia*. Most days were typical days, as with any family, except we shared our home with many others.

School, homework, visits to the doctor, work and play—we were doing our best to be effective, loving parents with all the issues that go on in growing active families. The demands of our visitors and guests added to this. Our kitchen was always an action point of our home. Our three guest bedrooms and bathroom were well used, but added pressure to daily life.

Late one night the phone rang.

"Pete, Bruce here. Time to talk?" His cheery greeting immediately took me back three years to the time when I had first met him on the dairy farm north of Wellington.

"Of course, Bruce. I still remember that beautiful spring morning and the enthusiastic welcome that you gave me as a complete stranger. I will never forget it. But that was just the beginning of a change of lifestyles. That first day, do you remember? Helen had a cup of tea and scones on the table before I could even explain why I was calling on you."

Bruce chuckled and needed no reminding of what happened then or after.

A year before leaving Wellington for Auckland to start our theology studies, we had invited Bruce and Helen to share a weekend with us on our small yacht we had moored near Picton in the Marlborough Sounds. It had been a memorable weekend. Between pulling in a few blue cod and getting lost in

The Tour adventure is about to begin! The picture on the front cover of the 2021 race book showed the sense of excitement and comaraderie among riders, while the map depicted the eight stages of the race.

The 2021 Tour of New Zealand was supported by: Ricoh, Honda, Vero, Avanti, Hynds, Downer, The Helicopter Line, and the Allan Scott family winery.

The 2021 Charity beneficiaries were: Heart Foundation, Tear Fund, Unicorn Foundation, Bikes in Schools, Child Cancer, and NZ Spinal Trust.

Arrowtown in autumn. The riders gather on the highest public road in New Zealand, ready for Stage 2 of the Tour of New Zealand 2021. Months of physical and mental preparation will be tested in the next two hours.

In the Tour, riding can get suddenly lonely. If the group you have been riding with are fast hill climbers, it's easy to get left behind. However, those lonely moments can be turned into learning moments. You can ride at your own pace and drink in the views of the mountains, suck in the cleanest air in the world, and know that with one pedal stroke after another you are still going to make it to the summit. Alternatively, you can stare at your speed on your Garmin, blame the race organisers for choosing such a testing route, excuse yourself for being ill-prepared, and curse the group you had been with for not waiting for you. It's your choice!

When riding in a group the kilometres race by under your wheels, and the effects of headwinds and fatigue are minimised. You feel new energy in your legs and are amazed at the collective power contained in the peloton. Each rider will spend just a minute or so in the lead then duck back for wind shelter by tucking in behind other riders where they use twenty percent less power. There is incredible comradeship and encouragement that flows within a team where every rider has the same end goal.

Haast Pass, April 2021. This stage of the Tour was accompanied by thunder claps and lightning flashes as a storm drove rain out of the skies like a fire hose on steroids.

GALLERY

Cape Reinga to Kaitaia, 2012. The riders are setting out on Stage 1 of the Tour. As in bike racing, how we prepare for the ride through the storms of life determines how much we will relish and be grateful for the sunshine moments we also encounter.

The very first race I entered as a schoolboy, I won easily. Being my first race, the handicapper gave me a ten-minute start ahead of the other riders in the 25 km race. I crossed the finish line still ten minutes ahead and felt like I had just won the Tour de France. A year later, in the 1960 Palmerston North to Wellington 160 km race, our group of ten started one hour ahead of the fast scratch riders, but it wasn't enough. Getting lost in the back streets as we came out of the city and losing about ten minutes, or so it seemed, didn't help! My team race car had trouble keeping up in places!

GALLERY

"*My grandfather (opposite) is the same age in this photo but he would not have dropped his gears in 1960!*"

Myles Yarrell, my grandson, drops his gears on a cool morning in the capital, Wellington, riding just three laps to raise $1400 for the Bikes in Schools charity.

Riding the Tour gives me a great feel for the stages and the spirit of the riders on the road. In 2015, we ran two simultaneous races—one in the South Island and one in the North Island, meeting in Wellington on day seven. In this picture I am giving a thumbs up. As my two race crews were doing such an awesome job, I was left free to ride every stage.

GALLERY

Tearfund is one of five charities that ride and also benefit from each Tour. A beautiful harmony between racing a bike and raising funds for charities drives the peloton forward into territory that other events rarely experience. The 160 riders in the 2021 Tour of New Zealand engaged with the charities at the nightly peloton parties, and during tour week raised $350,000 from their support networks of family, friends, and business colleagues. Selfless giving always unlocks unexpected doors and new opportunities, many that could change the direction of your life.

Olympian and Tour de France rider Julian Dean joined the Tour in 2017 as our celebrity guest. He rode the Tour with different groups on each stage. Laughing and joking and proffering advice with the riders, Julian would then effortlessly disappear up the road or mountain pass to catch up with the next group on the road and do the same all over again! Here he is pictured with Jilly, Pete, Simon and Guy Yarrell at the conclusion of the parliament criterium and Tour in 2017.

GALLERY

The Rt. Hon. Trevor Mallard, Speaker of the House, invites the Tour into New Zealand's parliament grounds for the final day criterium. The bronze statue of Richard Seddon, an early New Zealand Prime Minister, points skywards, as do the organisers in thanks to God at Tours' end for memories of climbing mountain passes, of clocking 70-80 kph once over the summit, of riding through storms of cascading rain beside instant waterfalls with ear-piercing thunder, of bellbirds singing in the morning, welcoming and encouraging the peloton as it passes by, and for safety and fun, and the health and fitness to compete.

the dark trying to find a mooring, we shared stories that always went back to the right-hand fork choice that Jilly and I had made, and the role of our Coach. Bruce and Helen had been attentive and fascinated.

Bruce clearly had some news and wanted to cut to the chase.

"Listen, Yarrell. Let me talk. We've sold our farm and are heading to Auckland."

"You have *what*? Bruce, that's incredible!"

"Yes, it is a migration of the Monk family north."

I listened carefully to Bruce's story, and it gripped me with feelings of humility and awe. Their farming days were about to change markedly. Their new responsibilities would be to lead churches under the wisdom and guidance of our Coach, and knowing Bruce and Helen's heartbeat, this decision would know no bounds.

Then Bruce got to the crunch.

"You could do with some more accommodation, and we would like to help. How about we give you a few hundred dollars as a sort of deposit, and you build some self-contained chalets and take some pressure off Jill?"

Bruce and Helen were true to their word.

We named the little complex after them, calling it *The Monkery*.

The Monkery changed everything for us. It included a separate kitchen for guests to prepare their own meals, plus we had a good-sized rumpus (or games) room. It became the hub that would also allow us to start a Friday night kids' club we called *Happy Club*.

The Yarrell kids—Simon, Juliet, Angela and Anna—had lots of school friends who didn't go to a Sunday School but would attend a raucous games and faith night every two weeks.

Bruce and Helen had no idea how much *The Monkery* would mean to us. As well, we were able to build two self-contained chalets beside *The Monkery*. This gave guests their own space and took pressure off our home.

Before the building of *The Monkery*, some of our guests' children would ask our children, "How long are you staying?" having no idea that they were Yarrells. They would look at our children and ask, almost in wonder, "Do you really live here all the time?"

The Monkery and the chalets gave us our home back.

Newcomer nights at Rua's, plus Friday's fortnightly *Happy Clubs* for the children's friends presented us the opportunity for a lot of creativity and conversations. We were in high spirits.

The next six years sped by. Our guests were introduced to the outdoors in many and various ways. Our Land Rover worked overtime, winding into the back country, criss-crossing rivers, and climbing otherwise inaccessible roads for high country barbecues or to explore gold mining sites long ago deserted. Riding horses on day-treks and sailing on one or other of the lakes provided the perfect backdrop for life-sharing conversations.

Many of the children from the small Arrowtown School were dropped off at *Koinonia* on Happy Club nights. Attendance rates were high. The children enjoyed the outdoor treasure hunts, exciting stories, yummy suppers, and fun games like egg and spoon races. Happy Club nights, we found later, turned into a double blessing allowing the children's parents to have fortnightly happy hours of their own, with friends at the Arrowtown pubs!

Our ten years at Lake Hayes was a life experience that money couldn't buy. Anything and everything could happen in a twenty-four hour period. We had decided that whoever knocked on our front door and wanted a bed, if we had the room, we would say yes—unless they were too troubled and might pose some risk to the family.

However, with our open home came situations and moments that showed up our inadequacies. Thankfully, help was at hand. John Clark and his wife Mary and family moved to Arrowtown in 1977. Dr John became a valued medical practitioner in Queenstown. Between consultations at the medical centre, tending to broken legs and arms from skiing accidents, or elderly tourists overdoing it in the heady mountain air and excitement of Queenstown, John and Mary graciously guided us with advice and professional help when required. We could refer any of our guests' medical issues to Dr John, and John and Mary would drop by some evenings to encourage and support us.

Curiously, the guests who enjoyed living by the swipe of a credit card to satisfy their every need were often the most unwilling to consider life beyond their own needs and wants. However, the guests who had been (or were going through) hard times and needed answers were far more receptive to direction. We came to realise that there was little we could do by using enthusiasm and ideas solely to encourage people who needed a change of direction and heart.

A pattern developed, with downs followed by ups, and when we felt we were not making headway with guests, a few days later a family would arrive and remind us how to laugh.

As the children approached their highschool years, we realised our next step was either boarding school or a relocation to Christchurch. We had given the open home experience our best, and now a bend in that right-hand track we had taken those years ago was rapidly approaching.

The year was 1983, and it was time for our family to move to a city where we could reconnect with the business world and the children could attend the highly regarded Middleton Grange School for their secondary education.

Two families had arrived in the latter years at Lake Hayes with a desire to help us at *Koinonia*. They had their own homes with guest accommodation close by. They also had willing hearts and different gifts from ours which would flourish in their own way amongst future guests. We were very grateful to a caring Catholic couple, who offered to live in our home in the short term to establish if they were able to handle the rigours of the lifestyle we had got used to.

It was a tearful day when we loaded up the car and trailer and headed out of Lake Hayes and Arrowtown for what we thought would be the last time. Who knew what lay ahead of us?

At dawn I made a cup of tea and walked slowly up the hill behind our house. I pushed through the wires of the fence Simon and I had built ten years previously, and found a spot to sit and reflect. My cup of tea had gone cold before I remembered to drink it, as for one final time I absorbed the beauty and stillness of the morning. The early rays of sunshine played on the mountaintops, defining the ridges and valleys above. They seemed to be saying to me a farewell but also a blessing for the future. Lake Hayes sat below like a giant's puddle without a ripple or boat to be seen. I found myself sad and full of memories.

From our home, this lake and mountain view had been framed by our front windows for the last decade. My thoughts and hopes, both realised and unfulfilled, confronted me: the horse rides to the gold-mining town of historic Macetown and beyond, the children rolling 'cigarettes' with newspaper and dry walnut leaves under the trees when we left them to rake the nuts up, the founding of the Wakatipu yacht club, and the first *'Bully Hayes'* race from Queenstown Bay to Kingston. I thought of the many guests who had stayed at *Koinonia*, and the sadness we felt when some left still lost in their thoughts that hobbled them. There were many more who told us how much they had felt uplifted and encouraged by their stay with us.

The love and spiritual energy of Rua Rout and her wise words and faith underwrote our five years of newcomers' nights. Our connections with

Queenstown business leaders, who we met with over regular luncheons, allowed us to share our lives. There was a cross-flow of ideas between the business community and our guests, which so many enjoyed. My heart was full of gratitude. For one last time I looked longingly at the mountains and the lake, shook my head, wiped my eyes, and returned to the packing up.

There was an adventure ahead—good schools for the children, full-time work again in the cut and thrust of the business world, new friends, and a house to buy when we sold our Lake Hayes home. *Think future*, I told myself.

It was a very long drive from Queenstown to Christchurch. On a good day towing a trailer, this journey would take seven hours, but a puncture in our trailer wheel (for which we had no spare tyre) halfway into the trip, plus four slightly sad, melancholy children and one Collie dog, made it an even longer day.

Arriving in Christchurch in the fading light and misty grey rain didn't lift our spirits. However, to our surprise, the rental house had lights on and was warm and welcoming. John Vargo had promised the key would be under the doormat and told us to check the pantry before buying any food.

John Vargo and Jim Bacon, were lecturers at Canterbury University, and along with their wives, had been guests at Lake Hayes with us a few months earlier. On hearing of our planned move to Christchurch, they promised to find us an affordable rental. They had chosen well and their generous kindness was evident and appreciated by a very tired family.

Simon, Juliet, Angela and Anna seemed excited about their new home. As we unpacked the trailer, there was a strange feeling of anticipation in the cool damp air that we couldn't explain. The house was furnished and the beds had electric blankets turned on by our good friends. Peeping into the small pantry we found it was stocked with groceries, and fresh milk was in the fridge.

We flopped into warm beds tired out but full of gratitude. What would day one in a big unfamiliar city bring us? Would I join a real estate company, or return to selling insurance? Whatever my choice, it had to be quick as it had to bring in some very needy cash.

I had every reason to be anxious, but didn't feel a worry in the world. We had just enough money to pay for our initial grocery needs and a week's rent. I dozed off to sleep confident that we were in the right place, and hoped like mad that the Coach had everything under control.

MY THOUGHTS

Investing ourselves and our home in others involved welcoming anyone who wished to stay with us. Each guest came, some with addictions, many others with deep hurts and languishing in bitterness and unforgiveness. In hindsight, if we qualified for recognition (which we certainly didn't want to) it was probably the equivalent to earning a master's degree and a doctorate over ten years in the midst of real life pressures as we learned the importance of perseverance.

STAGE 13

Back to basics

An AMP sales manager welcomed my phone call. "Is that the Peter Yarrell who used to work for AMP several years ago?" Jim Allan asked. "Time you came back into the fold, Pete. I will help you get established."

The thought of working a new territory the fourth time for the same company was loaded with negatives. I knew only the few people we'd become friends with when they'd stayed with us at Lake Hayes; otherwise, I had no contacts in Christchurch who could help me get established. However I did have the desire to work hard and knew that I would have to work long hours by day and into the evenings to build contacts. I could hardly afford the petrol to visit clients in their homes as we had no savings left. All our money was tied up in our unsold Lake Hayes house, and we had not asked our friends who were staying in it to pay rent.

When a real estate company approached me to see if I was interested in working with them, I had a choice to make. In the meantime, I worked hard at both.

I hardly knew Christchurch geographically. I felt at a disadvantage selling real estate in a city with which I was unfamiliar. In the end I passed my real estate exams and contacted a few buyers; however, no sales were forthcoming.

Going beyond any expectation of kindness towards us, our dear friends, the Vargos and the Bacons, asked me to arrange some insurance for them. Now I had a start. Jim Allan, my sales manager at AMP, promised me a retainer if I needed it to help us over the bump of the first twelve weeks with no commission.

Living in a city that was new to us created pressure in different and unexpected ways. Driving on unfamiliar streets following crumpled pages of maps felt like a confusing maze, particularly after dark and in foggy rain with no landmarks to refer to. Bank managers were almost as complicated to navigate and to win over!

"Jilly, my first commission cheque on the sales I made to the Vargos and the Bacons won't come through until Thursday," I said to her soon after we arrived. "When you buy groceries at the supermarket, give them a cheque and by the time the supermarket cashes it I should have enough money in the bank to honour it," I instructed my bewildered and worried wife.

After a furious day in the city insurance office phoning prospective clients and trying to make appointments, I drove home feeling worn out, with little to show for my efforts. Pleased to be home, I looked forward to some encouragement. But when I opened the front door I was surprised to hear Jilly sobbing in our bedroom.

"I went to the bank to cash the cheque and they said we had no money in our account. We have no food in our pantry for the children," Jilly said between sobs.

"Jilly, you have got it around the wrong way. I didn't say that. I said, 'Pay the supermarket with a cheque, and my commission payment should cover it on Thursday when they present it at the bank.'" I tried to reassure Jilly through her tears.

Driving my thirsty vehicle around Christchurch to attend appointments was an expense I could ill afford. The Land Rover was thirsty, clumsy, and a problem to park. I needed something cheap, economical and easy to park.

The salesman at the motorbike shop was keen to sell me a 50cc motor scooter that would solve all these problems. It was early June. Compared to

Queenstown, Christchurch was relatively warm.

"Because it is just 50ccs, you don't need a motorbike license," the salesman pointed out. "And yes, the small windscreen will stop the rain a bit."

I saw that I could put my briefcase between my legs on the running boards, and felt that with a warm jacket and a helmet, that would do it. My thirsty Land Rover could stay in the drive unless it was pouring with rain.

MY THOUGHTS

In Christchurch I was constantly getting lost. I tried to dismiss memories of my days in Wellington—then I had a 3.2 litre Jaguar, now I was riding a 50cc motor scooter; then, we lived in our own home by the beach, now we were in a rental house; then there were wealthy insurance-buying clients queuing up in a dairy-rich country north of Paraparaumu, now I was thrilled to arrange a car insurance policy on a second-hand Japanese import!

I knew that I was a different person. It did not occur to me to feel sorry for myself. I had inner resources now that helped me find the situation almost comical. Every day was an adventure. I had a confidence that my Coach would not leave us but guide us. There were signs that with persistence the peloton was again rolling forward and my fitness for selling would build week by week. I realised how much I loved the cut and thrust and challenge of business and how much I had missed it. The breeze was at my back and the sweat was once again on my face.

STAGE 14

Downhill and a tail wind

The sale of our home at Lake Hayes was a game-changer. Nine months after we arrived in Christchurch, new buyers made an acceptable offer and the 'Sale and Purchase documents' arrived for signing. At last, we could buy a home of our own in our new city and I was able to say goodbye to my Suzuki motor scooter. I needed to give it a final hug, as it had taken me to hundreds of homes safely and allowed me to begin to build a client and friend base that would serve us for the next twenty years.

Those months of rental housing turned out to be invaluable. The delays in the sale of our home, in hindsight, were very beneficial. The interim time had given us an understanding of the property market, as well as a settling-down period in our new city. I listened carefully to the advice of many new clients and friends. Location and sunshine hours and school zones were important to us. We attended open homes and gained a good knowledge of the market.

Eventually we found a house that fitted most of our criteria.

After months of looking, living out of suitcases and doing our best to settle into Christchurch, we were excited to receive a call from our friend and solicitor, Ken Lord, telling us the Queenstown house sale funds had been cleared and the key was under the doormat of our new home. It was a day we had waited for with anticipation beyond imagination. The Avon River ambled past the northern boundary of our new property and whilst the house entrance was close to the road, the section opened up towards the river with a rolling lawn and a little forest of trees the children couldn't wait to explore.

We felt so blessed. My insurance business gave me introductions to a cross-section of clients, many of whom would become friends, and my sales began to provide an income that paid the school fees and put bread on the table. We were experiencing Mark Knopfler's paraphrase of Psalm 23: "He leadeth me in pastures green. He gave us this day our daily bread and gasoline."

He also gave us some hand-picked neighbours.

"Hi, I am Cathy Brown from number 50. Just popped in to say hi. Our son Adam told us he's met Simon at school, and we realised we live in the same street."

David and Cathy were a significant gift from our Coach. Our new friendship would join us in adventures we had no idea of on our first meeting. The friendship between David and Cathy and Jilly and I and our families went deep. Sporting competitions between the families, regular tennis matches on the grass courts of Hagley Park, and discussions that led to us being invited onto the board of the school our children attended, drew us together. David's background in management put him in front of many of Canterbury's business leaders. He became a trusted friend and a mentor.

David played tennis like he played bridge. He always knew where to place the ball on the court. In a game of doubles, he would stretch the best of competitors. We played tennis under lights each week with two business colleagues and sometimes were unable to continue rallies as absurd shots and rallies dissolved us into laughter.

The four of us had business connections city-wide, and our discussions after our games gave David and me food for thought.

Over a coffee one morning I asked David a question. "Do you think we could put on the occasional luncheon for the business community where we'd be able to challenge and encourage business men and woman or mentor them? Would that be a good idea?" We sat in a café and David picked up a serviette.

I outlined to David how we'd done this in Queenstown and how much it meant to the businessmen and women who'd attended.

David always got it in one. He started to note names that came to mind on the serviette and before long realised we needed more serviettes. With that, the Christchurch Business Forum was born, and a date set for the first luncheon at The George hotel.

Shortly after the first luncheon, a client of mine introduced me to the owner of a private Auckland hotel. During our conversation, I found out that when in Auckland on tour, English pop star Cliff Richard had stayed at his hotel. The hotel owner told me how much Cliff enjoyed his tennis and that Cliff would always ask him to set up a match or two during his stay. He suggested that if I contacted Cliff's manager, he would likely recommend Cliff some tennis on the few days he was next in Christchurch.

This sounded big and I considered how best to bring it about.

There seemed to me to be one avenue I thought might work. When we first moved to Queenstown, Ralph and Robyn Webster had come to stay with us at *Koinonia*. Robyn had quickly become a good friend to Jilly. Ralph, head of Physical Education at Middleton Grange was also a Canterbury tennis champion. I felt he was the perfect person to set up a tennis match with Cliff Richard.

"Ralph, how do you feel about having a game of tennis with Cliff Richard?" The phone went quiet. I could imagine Ralph was wondering if he was hearing correctly or if I was being a bit stupid.

Ralph took a moment and replied in a tone of voice that searched my question. "Would I like a game of tennis with Cliff Richard?!"

Between concerts Cliff joined Ralph for tennis, and a relationship was built. David and I made up a doubles match and Cliff chatted to us over drinks between sets. Cliff willingly shared incredible stories from his extraordinary music and life moments. That gave us an idea. After one of our tennis games with Cliff, we asked him if he would be happy to speak at the next Christchurch Business Forum luncheon.

The date fitted with his week's concert programme. He unhesitatingly agreed.

The luncheon at Christchurch Town Hall's 'Limes Room' was filled to overflowing.

Ralph introduced Cliff with a couple of tennis stories and set the scene for the over-lunch chat.

The four hundred guests put their lunches to one side as Cliff humbly and sensitively shared moments from his life. His message was clear and simple. He talked about moments that became change-points in his life, including his meeting with Elvis Presley and the different roads they chose to walk down, and why he chose his road and journey. His sense of social responsibility was obvious with his support of Tearfund, and his compassionate heart resonated with our guests as he shared insights rarely heard.

Leaving the car park after the luncheon, David and I reflected on the day's events. The earlier tennis match with Cliff and Ralph was certainly high octane.

"You know David, I couldn't believe it was happening," Ralph said. "As I glanced to the far end of the court, there was Sir Cliff Richard in his tennis gear rocking from side to side awaiting my serve. I blinked. Was this really happening? Was I in fact serving tennis balls at one of the most legendary entertainers in the world?"

David nodded. "And then there was the lunch. What a turn-out! As I looked across the room at the faces of so many of our friends and listened to Cliff's talk and his journey of faith, I felt it was such a divine moment." David verbalised my feelings very well.

MY THOUGHTS

I thought back to the fork in the road experience I had at the age of twenty-seven where I faced a lifetime decision, and with little evidence or reassurance, took the fork in the road that seemed shrouded in mist and yet beckoned me to travel it in faith, rather than by sight. I felt humbled and inadequate, and at the same time deeply enriched by all the lessons and blessings the fifteen years since that critical decision moment had held. It was obvious to me that with all my struggles with human nature, and the bumps in the road I often experienced, my Coach wasn't an imagined God-theory; rather, He was a personal trainer extraordinary!

It is hard to convey in words the feelings we had after the luncheon. Perhaps they are best summed up by the motivator and author Ziggy Ziglar: "When you do your very best to make others successful you cannot avoid being successful yourself." I had felt enriched looking across at the faces of our business colleagues at that luncheon. I hoped that Cliff's words would resonate with many and encourage them, as they did me, to be successful in every sense of the word.

STAGE 15

Supporting each other

The Coast to Coast multisport race of 1995 was an event that seemed to be appropriate to enter to celebrate my fifty-first birthday.

Racing by foot, bike and kayak from the west coast of New Zealand to the east coast would be a formidable two-day challenge.

I needed a racing partner.

Though David Brown was brilliant at bridge, terrific at tennis, and very good at restoring classic cars, he would tell you himself that he is not a long-distance endurance athlete.

Just home from work, David looked relaxed and happy after his day in the office. I realised it was the perfect time to pounce! He was reading the Christchurch Press when I interrupted his thoughts. I was sure I knew the answer before I even asked the question. I had never seen him on a bike, paddling a kayak or running, except around a tennis court. His answer wouldn't even need words, it would just be a whimsical smile—he wouldn't waste his breath saying no.

"Ever thought of doing the Coast to Coast?" I began. Before he could answer, I continued, "I may enter it as a two-person team next February." There were nine months till then, and I needed a partner to run, ride and kayak on some of the legs. I could hardly look at David as I made my wild suggestion; it sounded so ridiculous.

David looked up from his evening paper and simply said, "Yes!"

"Sorry David, what did you say?"

"When do we start training then?" was David's next question.

"Are you for real, David? I mean this is serious stuff," I quickly pointed out, completely taken aback.

The following February, on the Kumara beach on the west coast of the South Island of New Zealand, the Brown/Yarrell team was poised at the start line, ready to go. Two over-fifty buddies with too much to do in life anyway should have known much better than to train for nine months for an event that they could never win. But it wasn't about winning. It was about competing together in an adventure that required more from us than we naturally had. We absolutely depended on each other to make it to the finish.

After my thirty-two kilometre stint of wading through rivers, boulder-hopping and running as fast as I could over Goat Pass in the Southern Alps, it was David's turn to paddle sixty-four kilometres down-river through white water and rock sections to the next transition, where I would cycle to the finish. The sight of Brownie (as I call him) paddling into the boulder-strewn transition at the end of his kayak leg left me emotional.

"I am here, I made it!" David was locked into his kayak with legs that had forgotten how to flex, and a bum that had gone way past numb. Officials took either arm and gently lifted Brownie to a stand-up position where he took what looked like the first steps of a twelve-month-old baby. He recounted his journey in gasps as he scrambled to the safety of the rocky Waimak Beach transition. How he'd kept his balance as he was tossed through the five kilometres in the cliff-sided, white-water-rapid section upriver, sounded like a high wire circus performance. David had been in his kayak for almost six hours! My bike ride into Christchurch, the final sixty-kilometre leg of the event, seemed relatively benign after David's drama in the kayak.

We had discovered how events draw people together, the fit and not-so-fit competing together in events where mutual respect, communication and natural friendships are enriched. For me, the Coast to Coast unlocked a thousand ideas. I found myself dreaming of organising competitive but achievable events targeted at everyday racers as well as the elite. The idea of charity-based events began to form in my head.

The idea of a run, bike, and paddle race taking in the natural topography of the city of Christchurch and environs made a lot of sense. We could plan to start and finish in the same location. A fast and flat run section would lead out of the city and onto an off-road mountain run, followed by a road bike stage to transition onto the Avon for the final kayak paddle. This would take competitors back to where they'd started. It made perfect sense, but it would take a lot of detailed planning.

The thought of a multi-sport event based in the heart of Christchurch City spun the wheels of everyone I talked to.

My enthusiasm levels went through the roof.

Our focus would be firstly on a route that was exciting and achievable. I did a 'reccy' of the course in a four-wheel drive. The race would start with a seventeen-kilometre run from Victoria Square to Lyttleton. Then we'd go off-road at Huntsbury to climb the Rapaki Track to the top of the Port Hills, then along the tops and over the ridges, then down into the port town, Lyttleton. The final leg would be a thirty-kilometre bike ride from Lyttleton to Kerrs Reach over Evans Pass, followed by a kayak up the river Avon to the finish back in Victoria Square.

My first part of the plan got a tick.

My next hurdle was to find a sponsor. It was important to me that I obtain a naming-rights sponsor. This would give the event a corporate relationship and provide seed funding for the start-up costs.

It was logical to make my first stop the insurance company I worked for.

When I received AMP's emailed answer to my submission for sponsorship, I hardly dared to open it. I held my breath. I then did what I often do when reading a reply to an email that I know is strategically important. I read it very quickly. This was some sort of nonsensical plan to protect myself from bad news. I knew that this email would either make or break the dream. AMP Life Insurance, had every reason to support health and fitness as it related so perfectly to longevity and well-being, values that insurance companies push to help reduce premature death claims.

The door in front of me swung open. AMP Marketing said "Yes!"

Now I had to look for clients, friends and family to support the event with me. I was bombarded with encouragement. Each member of the event team had to be totally reliable, capable and fun to work with. Everyone I asked enthusiastically and willingly volunteered to be on the event crew.

Little did I realise that many of the race crew I chose at that time would be working with me in events for the next twenty-five years.

The first 'City of Christchurch Multi Sport Race' was a step into the unknown. My forty marshals were augmented by twenty-five police who were rostered on for the duration of the event. Traffic lights along the main Colombo Street start area were turned onto a green wave by the council so that competitors were not stopped as they raced out from the start line at Cathedral Square. The police guided the competitors and overruled traffic lights in the outer suburbs, whilst my crew managed drink stations, provided medical backup, oversaw transitions, and ran timing checks and results.

Generosity with time and resources in the hands of competent people insured the event's success. TV coverage required a helicopter for filming, as the Rapaki track and Port Hills trails are off-road, making filming impossible for a camera crew on foot.

The volcanic hill scenery and feeling of exhilaration high above Christchurch city added to the excitement. Our plan to have a bagpiper standing on a rocky outcrop encouraging the runners on the mountain run could only be captured by a film crew in a helicopter. However, the cost of a helicopter for two hours' flying time would be about as much as the donation we hoped to make to the charity the event supported. It was either no helicopter and $10,000 for the charity, or a helicopter and at best a small donation for the charity.

It was then I thought of the great relationship I had with Terry and Phillipa Murdoch, owners of Christchurch Helicopters.

I had a plan.

The next morning saw me sitting in the small reception area at Christchurch Helicopters office, waiting to see Terry and Phillipa.

I was deep in thought. I knew that Terry and Phillipa were athletes themselves, and I also knew that they were incredibly thoughtful and kind. If there was any way that Terry could help us I knew he would, but I also felt concerned I would be trading on my friendship and therefore Terry would have difficulty saying no. I hate manipulation and would far rather keep Terry and Phillipa as friends than have the provision of a helicopter.

The secretary interrupted my thoughts. "Terry and Phillipa can see you now. Go on through."

"Well hello, Peter Yarrell. How are you? Not here to sell us insurance today?"

When Terry and Phillipa asked anybody "How are you?" they meant it. We spent the next ten minutes catching up and enjoying each other's company. A few months earlier, I had the pleasure of reviewing their life insurances. I learned that when Terry wasn't organising flight training for his many students, he'd be in the process of buying a new helicopter or flying one of his aircraft on 'another exciting mission'. However, despite all this he was always generous with his time and was a great listener.

"Terry, I have chatted with you about the AMP City of Christchurch multi-sport race that I organise. Well…"

Terry broke into my opener.

"Peter, don't ask. I'm not fit enough at the moment to compete. Running seventeen kilometres from Victoria Square to Lyttleton, let alone a bike ride over Evans Pass and then a kayak up the Avon river back to Victoria Sq…"

"No, Terry. I am asking for more." I could see Terry was smiling underneath his rejection and he bore no ill. "Terry, we have signed a film crew, and TV One have promised to run it the same night on their news and sport coverage…"

"…and you're asking me for a helicopter to cover the aerials?" Terry interrupted.

"What's the charity you're raising money for this year?" he went on without waiting for an answer. "What time do you want us at Victoria Square? We'll be there, Pete. The door will be off the helicopter, and we'll give your camera person a harness. Done! Oh, by the way, if you give Phillipa a free entry, we won't charge for the helicopter!"

"We can pay something, Terry!" I said, but Terry interrupted again and said there'd be no charge.

The 450 runners in the 1996 race gathered in Victoria Park at 7.30 a.m. for the race briefing. Springtime in Christchurch comes with the perfumes of new growth. It was a perfect, cool, clear morning.

My race director, Ralph Webster, gave the race brief and introduced the international model, Kirsteen Britten, to the competitors.

"Kirsteen has kindly offered to welcome you at the finish line with a bottle of Powerade, and if you are very lucky, a hug!"

A ripple of excitement followed by spontaneous clapping set the tone for a perfect day ahead.

It was start time. The distant beat of a helicopter's rotors, testimony to the reliability and kindness of Terry Murdoch, now hovered above us. Terry, with a cameraman harnessed in position on the doorless left-hand side of the aircraft, had everything covered.

The course ahead was set, marshals and police in place. The first rays of morning sunshine smiled upon the event, touching the spire of the cathedral adjacent to the start line in the city square. The speed bunnies at the front of the start line crouched slightly in anticipation of the start gun. The distant thumping from the rotors of Terry's helicopter and the super-quiet Sunday morning streets gave every competitor a very special feeling of anticipation.

As the starter's siren sounded, I found myself overcome by the moment. I thought of all the work, help, and hours of planning, the energy and commitment of the marshals dotted around the course, the film crew, the timing team, the medical support team. I felt deep gratitude welling up inside me. This was the first *AMP City of Christchurch Multi Sport Race*, and it would become a must-do annual event going forward.

MY THOUGHTS

That evening we gathered some of our crew and family to watch the TV One Sports News. Terry had made sure our camera crew got the best angles. The coverage was spectacular, recording even our bagpiper playing *Amazing Grace* (so appropriately!) while standing high on a rock beside the track as runners passed him. I thought of the 750 competitors and team members sitting with their families and friends watching the highlights of the event they'd just competed in.

I thought back to myself, aged seventeen in London and the experiences I was rescued out of. I thought back to the hundreds of guests at *Koinonia*, and what they taught us. I thought back to my hesitating choice of the right-hand path. I thought back to the cold wind I battled on my 50cc motor scooter on my early sales missions. I thought too about how blessed we were with each stage building on the next, and the Coach teaching me life lessons, giving me ideas, and slowly dispensing wisdom, patience, and strengthening endurance.

STAGE 16

A very high mountain road

It was a Saturday morning ride and a testing one at that. Our son, Simon, suggested a bike ride, and my desire for some family time overcame my desire for self-preservation. Our rides always took a similar pattern. He would start off chatting and riding around thirty-three kilometres per hour, and I would feel reasonably comfortable for the first thirty minutes which were pleasant enough. However, I would inevitably feel like a frog in a kettle. I would be slowly boiled as the speed increased, knowing full well that at the first minor hill, I would disappear out the back gasping, and Simon would have to sit up and wait for me.

However, this morning Simon was a little more relaxed. He even talked and rode beside me.

"Did you see that Prime Minister John Key is proposing bike tracks the length of New Zealand?"

I nodded.

"Well, why don't we organise a bike race the length of New Zealand, Dad?"

My mind spun faster than my wheels. "Like a New Zealand *Tour de France!*" I replied.

"Yes, maybe, but not at that level, more for riders like us. Competitive, yes, but most of us ride for health, relaxation, and comradery rather than hard-nosed racing."

It was 2010 and the idea just would not leave me. I began thinking about routes, logistics, crew, potential riders, dates, sponsors, charities. Everything sort of made sense. I needed very competent, trustworthy people to gather around the idea to see if it resonated.

I came up with three friends I'd learned to trust, all positive achievers. I knew they'd have the wisdom and courage to tell me to bin the idea if they thought it crazy.

I called my three friends together and made an appointment for coffee in Christchurch.

Mark Macdonald worked day and night in his family-owned trailer hire company. Rodger Searle was a founder of the popular trading newspaper, *Buy Sell and Exchange*, and Dave White was an expert in traffic management. They sat opposite, coffee in hand, studying me as I launched into the *Tour of New Zealand* idea that Simon and I had discussed. No one interrupted me. I depended on all three to capture the vision. Mark, Rodger and Dave would either 'flow and go' with it or they would 'block and beat' the idea out of me.

"Well, what do you think? Could this work, and would you work with me to make it happen?" I took a sip of my now-cold coffee and studied them for smiles or grimaces.

"Yep!" said Dave. Mark nodded. Rodger said, "It's a yes from me too. You've got three yes-es!"

The two hundred and fifty riders on the first *Tour of New Zealand* rolled in from countries all around the world and from points all around New Zealand. We offered as options to each rider a South Island course or a North Island course. The two events ran simultaneously over eight days with both pelotons meeting in Wellington on the final day for a criterium in the grounds of parliament, and a prizegiving. The current 'Speaker of the House' , The Rt. Hon Trevor Mallard, was a keen bike rider and kindly offered to host us, organising parliamentary security and resources, plus flags to fly on the flagpoles outside parliament, representing every nation competing.

Logistics were complicated. My hand-picked event crew of twenty-five from each island were now experienced at race organisation. They worked tirelessly to keep every rider safe and happy and were brilliant at solving problems.

Mike Pollok, the managing director of Ricoh NZ Ltd, and Dr Malcolm Legget of the Unicorn Foundation NZ, reminded each rider at the first of the nightly peloton parties that whilst the Tour was a race, it was so much more. It supported six hand-picked charities.

"When you pop your bike into the shed after your 600 kms of riding in one week's time, you'll have the satisfaction of knowing that those less fortunate than yourselves will have benefited as well," Mike explained. "We at Ricoh are proud to support the Tour, and apart from all the fun and adventure, you, the riders, will have raised tens of thousands of dollars from your network of family and friends. It will all go to the selected charities."

Mike and Malcolm explained that the Tour had two 'heart beats'—the ride (or race) itself, and the charity aspect of the event.

It would become the first of six biennial *Tours of New Zealand*.

Each Tour taught us lessons. Most riders understood that the race crew worked in a voluntary capacity and that we were a family of friends, with generosity of spirit helping to make each event even better than we'd planned.

Rod Oram, a business commentator, cyclist and friend, introduced me to Honda management in Auckland. For the first tour in 2012 Honda had lent Rod a car for his *Akina Foundation* team, which raises money for the *Bikes in Schools* charity. Honda then lent the Tour two lead cars for the 2013 event, one for the North Island and one for the South. At Tour-end, a team of five brothers from the Gardner family decided to buy the sign-written lead car for their much-loved widowed mother. This built a strong relationship between the Tour and Honda.

The following year, I received a phone call from Honda's marketing manager in Auckland, Lisa Campbell. "When are you and Coral (our Tour secretary) next up here from Christchurch on tour work?" Lisa asked.

It was the year between Tours, and Coral and I were busy with the new website and entry details. However, we had several sponsors and bike shops to meet up with in Auckland, so we planned a visit and booked some Air New Zealand tickets.

We were ushered into the board room at Honda's head office and waited a few minutes for Lisa and the CEO to join us.

After introductions, Honda's CEO, Mr Nobuya Sonoda, nudged us with a question.

"Is there anything else we could do here at Honda to assist you to be even more effective in fund raising for the charities?"

I was aware that Honda had strong social responsibility values, and we considered the generosity of Honda towards the tour already significant. My answer reflected this.

"If you are able to contribute a few prizes as well, like some Honda-badged umbrellas, that would be just amazing," I replied, feeling slightly concerned I was being a bit pushy.

"How would you like a car as well?" the CEO enquired. "We were thinking, if we donated a car and it was used in a draw for a rider raising money for one of the charities, would that be a good idea? It should feed through some energy and be an encouragement for the riders with their fundraising efforts!"

Coral and I glanced at each other in disbelief. *Was this a dream?* I wondered.

Thanks to the generosity of Honda NZ, *Tour 2015* saw the amount raised by riders for their charities increase by three hundred percent. The generosity and commitment of riders to the Tour was soon to be felt beyond our expectations.

At the final prizegiving in Wellington that year, Bruce Edgar, a New Zealand cricketer, was drawn as the winner of the Honda Jazz RS. The applause was loud and appreciative.

Bruce walked forward to the stage to receive the car keys. Lisa Campbell passed Bruce the keys to the $25,000 Honda prize. Bruce took the microphone and invited Beth Harper, Tearfund's relationship manager, to the stage. With a hug and a kiss, he passed the keys over to Tearfund, the charity for whom he'd chosen to ride.

"From me, with love," Bruce whispered quietly to Beth.

The stunned gathering rose to their feet. I sat still and wiped my eyes.

Encouraged by the fundraising stimulation the car caused, Honda continued supporting the event with the donation of a car.

The 2019 Tour included the honour of being invited into Parliament House by Trevor Mallard for the final prizegiving. In the Grand Hall, the 1890's hand-milled timber interior reverberates with New Zealand history. The two hundred and fifty riders and support crews settled in their seats as podium finishers were recognised, acknowledgements of sponsors made, and fun stories recounted. The climax once again brought Honda's Lisa Campbell to the stage. Stirring the rider's names in the bulging plastic bag Mike Pollok held out to her, Lisa acknowledged every individual rider's selflessness and hard work on and off the road. For the first time, Lisa herself had accompanied the Child Cancer riders on tour and spoke from first-hand experience.

"Is Katie Elliott here?" asked Lisa.

Katie and her husband, Jason, were from Aspen USA, riding the Tour for the second time. "You have just won a 2019 Honda Jazz RS," Lisa beamed from the stage. "Please come forward."

Katie threw back her head in laughter as she received the keys for the Honda. "Is Beth Harper from Tearfund here?" she giggled.

I thought, *Oh wow, not again…?!*

A dazed and amazed Beth stood beside Katie to receive, once again, the keys to the lead car. Several thousands of dollars were added in seconds to Katie's chosen tour charity, Tearfund.

MY THOUGHTS

I guessed that only five riders out of two hundred would pass the car on to the charity they rode for. These moments took us up mountains and kept us up there in the rarefied and unexpected air of generosity, selflessness and compassion. I will never forget those moments at the prizegiving after the clapping stopped. Nobody spoke for a few seconds. It was as if the Coach was present in person. Some would have been in awe, while others, knowing the prayer and sacrifice that many of our crew and riders engage in, would have seen it as a miracle moment.

STAGE 17

Preparation for the penultimate stage

The last hour of any long bike race can be the hour of extreme testing. You have an option. You can choose to ride at a comfortable pace and cruise over the finish line, unstressed physically. However, a competitive cyclist, one who wants to truly compete, would never consider that option. It is the last hour of a race that reveals everything about your fitness, your preparation, and the wisdom of your pre-race plan. That final hour exposes the weaknesses—your own, and those of your competitors. Winners work with this knowledge.

"Pete, what's next in life for you? What's on your bucket list?" contemporaries were asking.

"You've worked day and night for years. Come on, sit back, enjoy the fruit of your labours," they'd suggest. "How about a cruise down the Rhine? A long holiday in Europe? A bike ride across the USA?"

The thought of fulfilling lifelong desires was understandable. But for years now, I had 'ridden on the heights'. Life was just too exciting living beyond our comfort zone. Chugging down the Rhine surrounded by bucket-list pleasure seekers with cell phones firing photos around the planet, held little appeal.

I had learned that life was so much more than entertainment and pleasure and sucking the orange of personal satisfaction for the sake of it. I was anxious to discover the plans the Coach had for me in preparation for the penultimate stage. I knew there was always pain to achieve gain and that this stage was going to be by far the toughest. What I didn't know was where this stage was about to take me.

"Did you ever lose races by your own carelessness?" the Coach was asking. "You hadn't taken drinks and food at the right time and you simply ran out of energy? Or you underestimated the strength and cunning of your competitors and your preparation, fitness and self-discipline were simply inadequate? Maybe the hills were too long and a head wind too strong?"

I had to admit this was true, but I really didn't want to write about it.

"You should know by now that nothing happens that I don't allow, and everything is for a purpose." I knew that my Coach was right.

The Coach continued, "It's now time to write about your personal headwinds: what you learned when you tried, unsuccessfully, to become a member of parliament, your heart surgery, and other issues."

"I have a major problem here, Coach," I replied. "The stages I have ridden to this point have always had thrilling and unexpected outcomes. I know my *Born to Live* story has discouragements and heartache in the mix too, and I would prefer to leave those bits out."

"Wrong." The Coach was emphatic. "Think about it. These were the training rides that were preparing you for your final ride to the finish. You had so much more to learn," He added.

MY THOUGHTS

My mind went back again to when I was sixteen and competing in the Palmerston North to Wellington road race. I was extremely tired and still had thirty kilometres to ride, but then a strong southerly wind head-butted me. I had no food in my stomach and was so weak I struggled to catch a random jogger ahead. I remembered how I'd slumped to a standstill and held onto my bike for support and awaited a support car to take me to the finish.

STAGE 18

A wrong turn and a lesson hopefully learned

Selected as the candidate in 1990 for the New Zealand National Party in the electorate of Christchurch North, I was greener than grass politically, but full of enthusiasm, supported by a team of mates that worked tirelessly with Jilly and me to win the seat.

"But you lost." The Coach's voice sounded almost gleeful.

"Remember the day you were invited by the Prime Minister and members of parliament to attend the *Candidates meet the MPs* function in Wellington just before the election."

I remembered it very well.

"What do you remember?" The Coach was onto something.

I felt overawed by the occasion. Men and women I had only ever seen on television before, power brokers at the highest level, chatted to me warmly in a sort of unofficial welcome to a very exclusive club.

A senior party official kindly poured me a cup of coffee and introduced himself.

"I read that you are ahead in the polls in Christchurch North," he commented, giving me a nod of approval.

"Oh yes," I said, suddenly realising that people in high places were tuned in and closely watching my progress.

Surprised, I felt enthusiasm welling up. "The party by-line and slogan for the election so sums up my thinking," I told the official. *"Vote National for a decent society.* It says it in one."

He looked down at his coffee cup and replied, "I wouldn't get too excited about it."

I wondered where this was going. Looking up, he took a deep breath and continued. "It's only an advertising-generated tagline made up for the campaign. We think it's a great attention-getting selling point!"

I thanked him for the thought but found myself staring past him at a political world that suddenly seemed ugly, manipulative and coercive. I could think only of smoke and mirrors.

"And then what happened?" The Coach had some laughter in His voice.

The Labour Party which was then in government replaced Prime Minister Geoffrey Palmer four weeks prior to the election with Mike Moore, the popular member for Christchurch North.

A few weeks out from the election, with Mike's new position, the stakes shot through the roof. I now found myself not just trying to out-poll another member of parliament but the Prime Minister. He became unbeatable. The electorate now swarmed with television cameras, and new Prime Minister Mike Moore took every headline. The people of Christchurch North were delighted that the Prime Minister was from their electorate. In ten days, the polls had switched from positive to negative for me.

The intense feelings on election day are hard to describe. Your emotions are frayed. One moment you're thinking that the entire course of your life might change. The next moment you're wondering how to cope if you lose.

By 9.30 p.m. on election night the results spoke for themselves. Mike was re-elected, but it was close.

Strangely, however, the positive energy seemed hardly dinted. Our bustling election-night headquarters were emptying but my thoughts of disappointment were temporarily washed away by the words, hugs and laughter of our core team. Jilly and our daughter, Angela, had day and night helped me on our door-knocking campaign and letterbox drops. Together with many faithful friends we sat around a table and reminisced. We laughed through the recollections of our campaign opening gala-style night and how musician and lawyer Ken Lord pulled together a team of jazz musicians to entertain. My campaign chairman, David Brown, had told hilarious stories of the behind-the-scenes opening night laughs he'd had with two of our endorsing celebrities, an All-Black and a basketball legend. Brendan McNeil, the previous National Party candidate reminded us how Bruce's and Clyde's endorsements of me so impressed our keynote speaker, the Hon Winston Peters (later to become New Zealand's deputy Prime Minister) that he declared to the standing-room-only audience that he'd even vote for me himself!

A phone call from the Prime Minister interrupted the laughter. "Peter, I just wanted to say that you and your team ran a great campaign. Can I say too, that Yvonne and I have no children, and your daughter Angela who worked alongside you is a real credit to you. You're a lucky man."

I went to bed that night but didn't sleep much, my mind bombarded by what-if thoughts. We had come so close to winning. I dozed off at some hour, hoping that special votes still to be counted might change the result.

MY THOUGHTS

Mike Moore becoming Prime Minister crowded me out of becoming an MP. In hindsight the Coach had done a masterful job. The tools of many politicians are tools I never learned to use, nor did I want to. The experience of running an election campaign and mixing with political heavyweights showed me a side of life that appalled me, and yet the heady feelings of power, I noticed, attracted me as well. As I looked back, I could see power was almost an addiction and very compelling. The Coach knew better and didn't allow me to walk through that door. I was too immature, lacking in wisdom, and naive. He saved me again from myself.

I now understood that my Coach never showed His hand beyond His plan for the next day. Most times I could see His plan only retrospectively. One thing I began to understand was that regardless of previous miraculous interventions, faith in the Coach was a continual battle for me. I was appalled at my natural reactions, and the way I could so easily resort to my human nature when confronted by problems and difficulties.

When I mistook the road signs and took wrong turnings, away from the right fork I was meant to be riding, He always pulled me up and cleared the way for me to complete a U-turn. Yes, I had wasted a lot of energy but He produced the gels and drink to sustain me as I retraced my ride. This began to gnaw at me and frustrate me. I needed to save the energy that I had and not spend it on riding roads taking me nowhere. Yet even those experiences taught me lessons I couldn't learn by just reading the book or by going to club meetings. I found a fascination developing within me. I had come to a place in my life where it was becoming more important to me to build my relationship with my Coach than it was to win races.

The second headwind hit awhile later.

STAGE 19

A bypass, but not on the road

Bellbirds and Tui always greeted me on my early morning training rides on the coastal Queen Charlotte drive that joins the bays of the inner Marlborough Sounds. Applauding the gift of a new day, with their special songs of joy from deep in the forest, the bird life made my training rides very special. Striking shafts of sunlight gave the first kiss of warmth on my back as I pedalled as quickly as I could from bay to bay.

But this morning was different. Front of mind was the 100-kilometre Grape Ride just two months ahead, and my desire to compete at the level I had the year before. My sub-three-hour time had given me a medal in the over-65 category, and I was determined to equal or better that.

The first hill was hardly that, but enough for my lungs to deeply suck in the morning honeydew-filled air so that I could keep my Garmin in double digits. But something was different. Feeling as if a golf ball had hit me in the middle of my chest, I slowed to a pace that was just sufficient to keep me rolling forward without tipping off my bike. At the top of the small hill I pulled off the road and rested my arms and head on the handlebars and the pain stopped.

After I rode home, I decided not to alarm Jilly by mentioning it to her, so I popped my bike back in the garage and waited two days to hopefully recover.

Four months later nurses in Wellington hospital were beside my bed shaving my chest in preparation for a double bypass operation.

My Coach seemed to have taken absence without leave.

I awakened from the operation thankful that I was still alive, and reached under the bed covers and groped a tangle of tubes that were running out of my body from many places.

Life had changed and the next days in hospital gave me time to think, when I wasn't sleeping off the effects of serious anaesthetics, that is. There was a lot on my mind.

A year before the operation, I'd dreamed up the mechanics of a new race, a run, cycle and kayak event I called the *Queen Charlotte Classic*. There was a lot of work to do in the months ahead to prepare for this event.

Also, I had my insurance-broking business with hundreds of clients to look after, and we had family issues and demands that were complex.

As I lay in the hospital bed I found myself deep in thought.

I could hear a whisper from the Coach.

"At age fifteen you asked me to be your Coach, right? We've had many adventures together and I have had to intervene just to keep you alive!"

"Yes." My mind went back to the day I'd been about to leap off the train late at night when I'd woken from sleep and something had stopped me, then to the attack in London at the swimming pool. Both were quickly crowded out by other near-death moments, like the day my brother and I had gale-force, wind-blown cresting seas smashing into our small yacht when we were caught in an unforecasted storm in a rip, crossing the Cook Strait. I'd never known until now how we'd survived that! And now I'd survived open heart surgery.

Into my mind came memories of the many churches Jilly and I had attended.

Some of their leaders spoke about the Coach and that was fine, but few gave us the sense that they were allowing the Coach to speak through them. Attendance at the 'club' became more of a duty than an encounter with the Coach. And that was where everything got complicated. We would be torn between supporting the 'club', knowing the members were good people, and our unquenchable thirst to hear the still, quiet voice of the Coach. Pressures in life demanded wisdom beyond our own abilities. Life in the peloton was dynamic with demanding and dangerous forces working against us. Riding shoulder to shoulder on downhills at high speeds was about survival, and we needed confidence to make decisions that would thrill us and not spill us. We looked for fellow riders that understood this. Thankfully, we found some. When we did, we knew we belonged.

Medically, my recovery was progressing well. I had time to read, think and ponder. Back on the bike, I began to cautiously train for the next Grape Ride.

The Coach received many messages from me and now He attracted far more of my thoughts. I struggled to feel deserving of the care and attention He gave me but I was thankful and grateful. I read the book that I was given by Him at age fifteen with an almost unnatural hunger for every word. I became passionate for more interaction with the Coach and felt disappointment in myself that it took such an upheaval to have come to this point.

MY THOUGHTS

Everyone who has had serious surgery is 'given it' by the doctors prior to the operation. I vaguely remember the list of possible outcomes. The doctor started off on the gentle side. A person could suffer, I was told by the healthy confident doctor, from a list of unexpected but potential side effects of a bypass operation. This concluded with the final heart-stopper word: death. Whilst this sounds pretty serious, for me it was sort of funny as my interactions with my Coach had taken the sting out of death for me. However, in talking to other patients in the cardiac ward I noticed they often used words that sounded like bravado but essentially covered deep fears. I was thankful I had a profound peace.

As weeks passed, I dreamed and rested and slept my way back to a full recovery. One night I had a dream. Or was it a vision? It is said that young men dream dreams and old men have visions. Perhaps it was a mixture of both.

STAGE 20

The Valley of the Shadow of Death

The dream, which I have recorded below, was vivid and personal. I have added names and conversations to make it come alive for you. But I haven't altered the important details. Those I leave you to interpret for yourself.

My Coach sat in the team car, roadside. I pulled up beside Him on my bike. His front passenger window was already open.

"Have you got a minute to talk?" I asked.

"Absolutely," my Coach replied.

"Well, I suspect it was you who planned for me to ride the last few years through those ghastly roadworks, sometimes my wheels losing traction and almost tipping me off in the patches of thick gravel."

I wasn't accusing Him but I felt emboldened to raise the subject.

My Coach leaned forward and pushed the stop button on the car dashboard. A strange silence enveloped the scene. It was a very informal setting to be talking deeply, albeit through the side window of the team car, leaning on my handlebars, but these thoughts had been brooding in my mind for a long time.

My Coach didn't show any sign of surprise at my observation.

"With respect, there are a number of other coaches that I could work with, and chatting to some riders coached by them, they suggest I should look at changing coaches." I felt terrible saying this, but I was getting desperate.

"Pete, you always have the freedom to be coached by whomever you choose." I didn't think my Coach noticed it, but at that moment I felt completely ashamed of myself.

"Reflect for a moment, Pete. These riders you speak of, how are they doing?"

I didn't want to go there, and lost for words I stared down at my handlebars.

I ranked my Coach very highly and had done so for years. My mind swam with pictures from the past. My life had been crazy. The rescue missions and restoration work He performed when I fell off my bike were too many to recall. He had let me loose enough to do some idiot things, and then reined me in to help me learn from my own mistakes.

Without words, it dawned on me that the roadwork sections of the previous years were preparation for something on the Tour that was just about to begin. Thankfulness welled up inside me and replaced the negative feelings that I had blurted out to my Coach a few moments before.

Without any sign of frustration or the slightest indication of disappointment with me, He concluded our talk and passed me an envelope and a backpack.

"You have now done enough preparation and training to ride up the mountain, Pete," He said. "Just a word of guidance as to what is ahead. You will find that after about thirty kilometres of serious climbing you will arrive at the city in the valley of the shadow of death. You will need to refresh yourself there as your destination is a further climb that can take days unless you discipline yourself to take one pedal stroke at a time and be patient. Some give up and go back to the valley."

My Coach explained only as much as I needed to know, then stopped abruptly. He seemed to be a bit choked up.

Before I could ask any questions, the passenger window silently slid shut and my last memory of my Coach was a growl from the twin exhaust pipes of the team car and a brief wave as it headed on skywards.

I turned to look in the direction the team car drove and my heart almost stopped. Ahead was a mountain of all mountains. The top of the mountain was completely obscured by high clouds and the only road I could see was the beginning of a zigzag that led to the 'valley of the shadow of death', as my Coach called it.

In my dream (or vision), I carefully zipped up the envelope into the backpack, then topped up my water bottles in a fast flowing stream by the roadside, and clipped my shoes to the pedals.

The zigzag road at the base of the climb was not as steep as it looked but once it got onto the climb proper, I sucked my water bottles dry. It was late in the day when the road at last flattened out, and the noise of the busy city was evident even before it came into sight. I was hungry, thirsty and hot, and I needed a bed.

On both sides of the road that led into the attractive city was a good selection of modern hotels at what looked like ridiculously low prices.

I checked into one that advertised itself at fifteen dollars a night.

I took my key and found the room on the second floor. It had space for my bike in the entrance area and a good view across the city to lakes and mountains in the distance.

Glancing in the one mirror beside the bed I noticed my sweat-covered face and lines of salt around my mouth. I'd forgotten to ask the receptionist if the room had an ensuite and realised the room I had passed at the top of the stairs that was signed shower and bathroom was a communal one. I began to understand why the room rate was so cheap.

With my towel around my waist and my soap and key in my free hand I clattered down the wooden hallway in my bike shoes to the bathroom.

A voice from the bedroom between my room and the bathroom called out.

"Who is it?"

I quickly learned that it was owned by a fellow bike rider who, upon opening his door, introduced himself as Marcus.

"The showers are all on a two-minute timer," Marcus informed me.

I thanked him, and no sooner had he appeared than he disappeared back into his room. I thought he was probably a bit miffed that I had just beaten him to the one shower in the vicinity and he would have to wait. The two-minute shower was exactly as he warned me. It was a duck-in and duck-out version, but it was also warm, wet and did the job, so Marcus didn't have to wait long.

Dinner was served at 6.30 p.m. There must have been twenty tables in the dining room, but I was the only diner—that is, until Marcus arrived.

"Do you mind if I sit with you?"

I was pleased for his company and later was amazed at how much I learned in the thirty minutes that followed as I invited him to tell me about himself.

He started off by giving me his background. He told me that he had arrived in the city three years previously and like me had stopped to gain refreshment and rest for five or six nights before hitting the longer serious climb to the summit. His Coach had warned him, as He warned me, of the need to be fresh in body and mind before heading higher.

"I was planning to leave, but after a few days I was offered a highly paid government job and found the city had much of what I wanted in life. But let me hasten to add there are some important exceptions."

Marcus frowned. In essence he told me three things I needed to know:

1. If I stayed more than a few days I would probably end up like him and become a permanent resident of the valley of the shadow of death. He had chosen to stay after he found that the city had everything from free health care, superannuation subsidies and high-paid government jobs. It was also very ordered and clean, and police rigidly enforced the law.

2. There were some downsides. The state government imposed heavy taxes and tracked everybody with cctv cameras wherever possible. They also had access to everyone's bank records, and required everyone to sign in with QR codes when they entered any building or public place. Basically, the state had replaced God. Marcus said they knew when you were at home, where you worked, and when you were out and about.

3. I would soon realise that the whole city was controlled by the state. If ever it felt it was losing control, it used fear backed by police action to regain its hold. Surprisingly, the citizens obeyed almost without question.

Marcus explained over dessert that I should dress inconspicuously and tour the valley with my eyes wide open. He recommended seeing the city by tram over the next few days, pay with cash, and not tell a soul of my plan to head on up the mountain to the summit or about my relationship with the Coach. Christianity was mocked, he said, and any believers cancelled.

I felt he was honest and trustworthy, so I asked him what his job was.

"I will trust you to tell no one. I work for the government as a cyber security specialist, and I share the same faith as you, but unlike yourself, I am compromised. We have a sort of underground church with a number of friends, but we always move around café to café."

We shook hands and planned to have dinner together at a restaurant Marcus recommended the next night.

The next morning couldn't come quick enough. I found a café for breakfast and then caught an early tram for the city centre.

It was a spectacular day. On the tram, a woman by the name of Samantha introduced herself to me. Sitting beside her, she somehow worked out that I was a visitor. When she asked me if I would like a commentary about the city from the tram, I readily agreed. She filled me in to a level of detail I would never have otherwise known. As I went to get off the tram she told me it was her stop too. She pointed to the medical practice she was a receptionist in, and then looked at her watch.

"I have ten minutes before I am due at work," she said. "Do you want to sit in the sun and we can finish our conversation? Just call me Sam," she added.

I told her my name was Peter said she could call me Pete.

Sam almost repeated what Marcus had told me the night before. I noticed she glanced around a lot and spoke quietly. I thought it safe to tell her of my plans to ride to the summit in the next few days.

"Pete, you shouldn't tell anyone that," Samantha said. "You are a lucky man because I have already been up to the summit, and I can tell that you are so different from the people that live in this city. That was why I opened up the conversation on the tram."

Before I could ask her about the summit, I looked and she was gone. She turned and gave me a secretive little wave as she disappeared through the door into her work.

The dinner with Marcus later that evening answered a lot more questions for me. Though I had only toured the city for the day, I could completely understand why he had chosen to put down his roots.

He told me that our talk together the night before had reinvigorated him to make plans to ride up to the summit. But I could see he was struggling with some inner thoughts.

I probed, as I hoped it may help him if he could articulate his thoughts.

It turned out that he loved fast cars and had taken on a huge debt to pay for his Lamborghini. He told me he was locked into his work as his debt repayments on the car were very high. And the option to sell his Lambo? Well, that was unthinkable.

Marcus looked slightly edgy and embarrassed. "Pete, the Lambo gives us the opportunity to indulge me and my girlfriend in what we call *Friday night sport in the city,*" he said. I wasn't sure where this was going so just waited for Marcus to continue.

"We dress up in our best casual gear and as quietly as we can, we rumble our 540 horse-powered Lambo down the main streets of town. The city really hums on a Friday night and the pedestrian crossings are packed. If we are lucky enough to be the first car off the rank, I tickle the accelerator as the lights turn from red to orange to green. With the streets clear ahead, I kick the accelerator to the floor, and the growl from the twin turbos reverberates off the shopfronts and high rise buildings as we hurtle off the white line while crowds look on. All they see is two serious faces with eyes covered by Gucci sunnies, but the satisfaction we feel makes waiting a whole week to unleash the beast so worthwhile." Marcus paused, then corrected himself. "I mean, the satisfaction we felt."

"Felt? Marcus what do you mean?" I queried.

"Well, Pete, it used to be a great night out for Barbara and me but for some reason we are beginning to feel that we have been there and done that. It seems just showy now and we don't get the kicks anymore."

I could see in Marcus' body language a loss of satisfaction and realised he ached for the purpose and destiny he sensed in me.

I had learned a lot from Marcus over dinner and wondered if one day a door would open that would allow us to relate more closely. We shook hands and parted. I think we both had a desire to take our chat to another level, but now wasn't the time.

I spent the next three days or so peering out the windows of the free trams. I visited museums and read the fascinating history of the city in the central library. The money I discovered in the envelope the Coach gave me after our brief chat at the bottom of the mountain allowed me to visit most of the attractions and eat well. On the fourth morning, I planned a very early start hoping I could slip out of town without being noticed.

A pleasant early morning breeze cupped my back as I rode the tree-lined avenue leading to the start of the summit road. It was cool but not cold, and I could see the first light in the mountains turning the night sky a lighter blue as I turned onto the first slopes of the climb ahead.

I didn't look up the mountain, as I was well aware of the long hard ride in front of me. I just drank from my water bottles, nibbled on some energy bars, and spent the next hours thinking about the three days just passed.

My mind went back to the words that Marcus used to warn me, over dinner, on my first day at the hotel. What I discovered understated the situation. To remember everything in detail, I started to recall every event as it happened. Remembering Marcus' words, I had paid careful attention to watch out for prying cameras. I had been surprised at first, as I couldn't see any on the tram, but then I noticed what looked like buttons grouped together but with each one on a tiny stalk moving very slowly in a rotating arc.

From the tram window I had watched in amazement as queues of residents were marshalled, just as Marcus had told me, in the sort of cattle grids that airports use for security screening. But these people were trying to buy tickets to get into 'flesh and flash night and day clubs' as they described them. Casinos and the pub patrons were made to go through the same screening procedures at entrances. There was little laughter and a strong police presence. On and off at every stop the trams would empty and then rapidly fill again.

It was both fascinating and concerning, observing the faces of the people lost in inner thoughts, many just staring into nowhere and devoid of emotion. Some stumbled their way onto the tram looking beaten and lost, and I knew why. I could feel it like I could almost touch it. There was a power, a dark power of entrapment, and I could feel it compelling me as well. I found myself wanting to also get off the tram and heard a voice saying to me, "It's okay to join them; satisfy your curiosity, there is nothing wrong with that."

I felt dirty even thinking about it. A strong seductive spirit was at work.

I mused further. There were contrasts—parks, golf courses, yachts on lakes, bike tracks, and super flash cars towing boats. To be fair, some people in the city looked like they were having some fun and enjoying themselves.

Samantha had summed it up well. "If you comply and don't question the rules and directions of the State authorities, life can be pretty good here. However, if you dig a bit deeper, the emptiness and loneliness in this city generally, is ugly and tragic."

That sounded like shocking manipulation and control to me.

"If people aren't coming into our medical centre because they have depression or an addiction to drugs or alcohol, they are coming in for stress-related illnesses or sexually transmitted diseases," Samantha had told me.

"The system in this city, for all its government sweet talk and compliance rules, is sadly soulless and bankrupt. People here look to entertainment and sport to fill the void that was once filled with faith, hope and respect for God's laws. To control everyone, we have rules and laws that are forever changing and that box everyone in with threats and punishments designed to frighten."

I remembered almost word for word our conversation and it summarized exactly what I had observed.

The summit road wound around the face of a ridge. It was way past lunch time. I remembered the words of my Coach advising me I must stop only briefly and just to keep pushing down one pedal after another, or I would never make it. However, I knew He would want me to have a short lunch break.

I looked at my Garmin and was surprised to find that my thoughts had occupied me far longer than I realised. It was almost 3 p.m. and my Garmin also told me that I had been riding for eight hours. Without even realising it, my subconscious mind had worked out that the eight hours I had already spent riding to the summit, which still hadn't come into sight, would equate to just a couple of hours riding back down the mountain. From the rock I sat on, eating my lunch, I could just make out the 'valley of the shadow of death' below.

I found myself thinking about Marcus and Samantha. Yes, they were right—that city was pretty amazing, but a flood of apprehension began to almost torment me.

My Coach had invited me to the summit, yet I realised He hadn't told me what to expect when I reached it, or the benefits and gain for all the pain. I ate my remaining banana and stared back down at the city in the distance below. The option was there. *Marcus and Samantha had chosen to stay, and they had a relationship with the Coach,* I pondered.

I don't know what changed my mind about heading back down the mountain but to my surprise I found myself on my bike and again heading skywards. My brain said yes, go back, but my spirit didn't. I was unsure why, but my spirit won. Rounding the next corner, I looked to my right and got my first glimpse of the summit.

It is hard to describe in words what this did to me. Energy and excitement joined hands, and though the next thousand or so vertical metres would demand my last drop of sweat, suddenly every pedal stroke had a new purpose. The last hundred metres and the sight of the parked team car and my Coach standing beside it, took me into a surreal moment that removed every ounce of lactic acid from my legs and sped me to the side of my Coach. Through my misted-up, wrap-around sunglasses, I noticed tears in His eyes.

"Look around you, Pete. Wipe the beads of sweat from your eyes and take a moment to get your breath." My Coach hugged me.

Wiping my eyes, I couldn't believe what I was seeing. I felt I was looking down from above the planet, and the creation below revealed a beauty and peacefulness that made every pedal stroke and drop of sweat worth everything I gave on the ride up the mountain.

STAGE 21

A face-to-face with my Coach

It seemed enough to have made it to the summit, but then my Coach really caught me by surprise. He put his arm around my shoulder and gestured towards some smoke that lazily drifted heavenward from a rock fireplace near the side of the road.

"Let's chat further, Peter."

I felt unworthy and hesitant. If my Coach knew how close I had come to extending my stay in the valley below and how captivated I'd been with the city and the couple I'd met, He would have been disappointed in me. When I experienced the pull of darkness on the tram that day and was not repelled by it, but drawn into it, I felt ashamed of myself. My motivations and my actions were under a spotlight that would leave nothing hidden. I had nowhere to go.

We sat on a couple of camp-style chairs. I stared into the fire, which saved me having to look at my Coach's face.

"Peter, you met up with Marcus and Samantha in the city…"

I couldn't believe He said that. I glanced up and found myself looking straight into my Coach's eyes. They had not a flicker of anything in them that reflected any disappointment in me, or condemnation of me.

"Well, yes Coach, I did." My brain was running faster than it ever had.

He leaned forward. He didn't take His eyes off me, and I was suddenly at ease looking into His. "Sam and Marcus do a lot of work in the city for me, and shall we say, it was no coincidence that you met them both."

I was completely disarmed.

"But, Coach!" I blurted out. "If you organised that, you must have organised the tram trips too, and you'd know my heart and my thoughts."

"Why are you surprised Peter?"

I couldn't answer. I looked back down at the fire. I felt confounded and exposed, but not judged.

"Peter, you have come so far and you still don't understand?" Without waiting for an answer, He continued. "I know that you think that life is a bit random, and you just bump into people and find circumstances that make things happen. That is understandable. However, what you see as coincidence and chance are not that. We have a lot to talk about. You and I have been together for a long time now," my Coach reminded me.

He stopped there, and I closed my eyes and stilled my heart. Human words could not answer my questions nor could philosophy or a brilliant mind.

I felt to take off my bike shoes… it seemed that all around me was holy ground.

I thought long and hard. Questions flooded my thoughts.

"All this is beyond my understanding, Coach. Why me? I feel everything is so undeserved. Sometimes, I feel so arrogant, telling friends that have chosen other coaches about your involvement with me."

I took a deep breath. I was amazed. Our face-to-face was far more of a fireside chat between two friends than a formal meeting between me and my Coach.

I went to tell Him about my experiences of the last fourteen years then realised this was ridiculous and unnecessary because He knew already! He had planned everything!

"Pete, everyone, not just you, has an inextinguishable desire to be self-centred.

Because of my relationship with you, you feel that disconnect strongly, and it keeps us close. However, continual self-absorption causes a 'leprosy of the mind'. The self-absorbed often make themselves the centre of their thinking, which determines every decision that they make," my Coach explained.

I knew that was true, but I had never quite understood why.

"Do you know much about leprosy, Pete?"

"I have read that people with leprosy can put their hand in a fire and will suffer horrendous burns and yet not feel a thing," I replied.

"True," my Coach agreed. "A person that doesn't listen to and obey their conscience will soon develop leprosy of the mind. By that I mean, just like the leprous hand in the fire, they become oblivious to the damage they are doing to the people around them."

"So, there is a progression in developing mind leprosy?"

"Yes, Pete. It begins as a rationalised thought, then clothes itself in reason, justifies itself by comparison, and is permeated with half-truths to gain acceptance. Its reference point is the benefiting of self, and it concludes by establishing a new normal. With repetition this process slowly replaces the voice of conscience and truth."

"I've never had this explained to me before," I observed.

"And that is why I asked you about leprosy, Pete. Have you ever seen a picture of the limbs of a person with this disease? A dead conscience is more damaging than leprosy is to the body. It is hidden within and destroys from without."

I had never thought of that.

My Coach, continued. "Your conscience is the repair kit for life. When a rim on a bike wheel starts running on the tarmac because of a puncture, it is screaming at you to stop to fix the puncture. If you ignore this, you will damage your rim and go nowhere fast. In the same way, when you excuse your failings and ignore your conscience, you are on a self-damaging journey with consequences you were not designed for."

"Nobody talks about this, Coach."

"The reason is predictable. No one has ever seen a conscience. A doctor cannot put a camera up your groin to check your conscience."

I'd never thought of this, but my Coach made a good point.

"Think about the ride you have just done up the mountain," He said. "Why did you take so long, Pete?"

I had thought about that on the ride. The forces of gravity had worked against me for hours, slowing me to a walking pace at times.

"Did you actually see these forces of gravity? Were there images or signs on the roadside, or identifiable colours in the air? No, of course not! Gravity is present but unseen. Only the effects are noticed."

My Coach continued. "The forces of evil have a similarity with the forces of gravity. They are unseen, but ever present. A tender, working conscience identifies the wrong, and it causes a healthy guilt to engulf and redirect, to put right the wrong. If the conscience isn't active, then there is a resigned acceptance of dysfunction and the wrong is internally justified and excused. In effect, your ride in life turns into a long walk, and you need to put your bike on your shoulder and carry it to the finish. Life wasn't designed to be like that."

I completely understood.

"One last question, then Coach," I asked. "Some of my friends are carrying or pushing their otherwise magnificent bikes along the road edge. Many have helped me at different times. Can they get their punctures fixed and their tyres pumped up so they can ride again?"

"Pete, if only it was just a few of your friends that had this problem. But friends or not, any person who invites me to be their Coach and sort their puncture will have their consciences rebooted, their futures redefined, and their peace restored."

I knew exactly what the Coach meant.

I clipped my shoes back into the pedals. My Coach had given me a lot to think about. As I left the summit and hit the steeper downhills, my bike touched eighty kilometres per hour. I thought of the pain of the climb I had been through coming up the mountain. It now seemed like an age ago. My bike felt alive beneath me. I swooped the corners, drinking in the views which I had missed on the climb up. Songs of joy filled my head and heart, and I felt freedom and wisdom and energy that was intoxicating. What an incredible stage!

My ride up the mountain earlier had given me the time and solitude I needed to think through what I had learned from my few days in the city of the shadow of death.

As I continued in my state of exhilaration on the long downhill ride I felt compelled to stop and unpack my mind. Even though it seemed I was alone on the mountain I didn't feel slightly lonely. The Coach was with me, and the Coach's words hung in my mind. In the mountain air, I felt I could almost physically touch them.

I squeezed my brake levers. A patch of mountain heather beckoned me roadside. I had never sat on a carpet of young heather before, and I was pleasantly surprised. It felt so soft and welcoming. I was in no hurry. I needed to process the tumbling thoughts that filled my head. Time stood still for me. I could never be the same.

I closed my eyes and buried my head in my hands. The ramifications of my meeting with my Coach were far-reaching. Who would believe me if I told them?

I don't know how long it took me to open my eyes and feast on the views. The clock of time had become completely irrelevant. The dials on my conscience seemed to have been adjusted to full blast and I began to see different routes to take on the next stages of the Tour.

I felt my legs and arms shuddering, yet I wasn't even slightly cold. I just needed my Coach to help, as I felt I couldn't do it alone.

"Pete, fear has replaced faith on the planet, and you are being sent back to write in the pages of your book a revelation I will bring you at the right time. There will be a cost you would prefer not to pay. But I will carry you through. At the top of the mountain we talked about the gift everyone receives—namely, a conscience, and the need to listen and obey it. Now I am going to take you to the brink. I am inviting you beyond the grave, and as I taught you, just pay close attention and listen to your conscience."

My Coach always had His plans and I had learned I could trust Him. I was disappointed when He picked up my bike, held it for me to mount, and pointed it down the mountain road.

"Can't I stay with you on the mountain, Coach? I love this."

"No, Pete. Ahead is another adventure. You have more stages to ride, and you will find that many in the peloton will look to you for guidance. You will ride well, as you work on your fitness, and you will be a good buddy to the riders I put you beside."

It was two hours before sunset and there was not a cloud in the sky. The thought of catching up with Marcus and Samantha and telling them of my ride up the mountain and my conversation at the top made the ride down to the city turn into a race against the sun setting.

I was still planning a riding group in my head when I arrived on the outskirts of the city. I was thankful for the street lighting that had switched on just in time to lead me back to the fifteen-dollar-a-night hotel.

MY THOUGHTS

Writing the vision gave me awareness and fresh impetus for what lay ahead. I find myself reading and rereading it, and reflecting on it in awe. Where the words came from or how they were formed, is beyond me. What I do know is that the Coach whispered them into being, and I recorded them.

STAGE 22

Who is your "Lead Out" rider?

It all went so smoothly.

It was November. We had an apartment we could holiday in at Queenstown. We also had a window of time available, and the Prado parked in the garage looked ready for a holiday as well. As we packed and headed south we had no idea that exactly two years later we would be not just packing the Prado with some overnight essentials, but we would be packing two furniture trucks and leaving for Queenstown permanently.

The real estate windows in Queenstown always have compelling photos of properties that trigger dreams of relocation, but nothing in them that November holiday even began to spin our wheels. However, the morning we planned to return home, an advertisement in a real estate magazine caught my eye. It pictured two acres of bare land on a thousand-acre farm called Threepwood, near Lake Hayes.

Five hours later, Jilly and I could hardly believe our eyes. The sun-drenched property eyeballed the Coronet Peak ski field. It sloped down to a wetland area to a small stream. Facing west, we had 180-degree views of the mountain ranges with rolling farmland in the foreground. The property was just five minutes from Arrowtown and Lake Hayes, and was only a one-minute ride from a trail that joined all the local mountain bike trails that criss-cross the Wakatipu basin.

We stood on the building site, now scraped and formed by the digger at the end of an eighty meter drive. We had one hundred and sixty trees to plant and irrigate, plus a three hundred square-metre home to build. We felt from the day we 'discovered' the property that our Coach was intimately involved.

Crazy coincidences favoured every move we made. Just hours before our settlement payment was to be made, Maria, our thoughtful and trustworthy bank manager, rang confirming bridging finance. We signed up our building company, Cook Brothers, and they did everything they said they would do and more.

One late afternoon, with only the company of a hawk gliding above and pukeko foraging on the wetlands below, I stood on the building platform in a complete hush of total silence and stillness. My thoughts went to the many moments of guidance that my Coach had whispered into my ear over years past, and I felt a warmth of energy envelop me. There was a whisper in my ear that went something like this:

Coach: Remember the words I gave you in 1971? You were sitting in your Mini reading the book written by Edith Schaeffer.

Me: That was a day I will never forget.

Coach: The words you read, what were they?

Me: Come let us go up to the mountain of the Lord and to the house of our God. He will teach us of His ways so that we may walk in His paths.

Coach: And . . . ?

The conversation ended there. My Coach didn't need to state the obvious. I had previously considered that those words were fulfilled in the years we were at *Koinonia*. But now I realised they were being fulfilled in front of my eyes. It was an awesome and intimate moment with the Divine.

I felt my Coach had another adventure ahead. As always, He wouldn't detail it. That would be for us to discover.

Living in an insulated garage for twelve months whilst our house was being constructed would keep us close to the action and available to answer the many questions our project manager asked of us. We waited for the plumber to run the water supply and install a toilet, and for the electrician to hook up some power. In a few weeks (and well before winter) it was all in place.

MY THOUGHTS

Our home is now built. As I write, the wood fire licks flames into the chimney, snow tumbles out of the sky, larch trees turn white, and a hawk cruises just above the tree line looking for some morning tea.

I think back to the day that my friend Des questioned me sixty years ago with the words, "If an atomic bomb lands on you today, do you think that you will now go to heaven instead of hell?" As I have embarked on each stage of the 'Tour of Life', I have found that things aren't quite that simple.

Should we have taken the left-hand branch on the road all those years ago? I am sure things would have worked out, but I am not sure I would have written *Born to Live*. Thankfully, my Coach does not have a one-bike-fits-all stable of bikes. Every bike is tailor-made for each rider that joins the peloton.

The most exciting moments of any bike race is what lies ahead. For the many who follow professional bike races, they know that the winner of the sprint over the finish line is never normally the rider that leads out at the front. The designated sprinter shelters behind what is known as the 'lead out rider', and with just a few metres to go, launches himself or herself across the finish line to win. The trick is to know the right person to follow, draft behind that person, and then hang onto that position at about 65 kph when every other rider is trying to do the same thing!

Similarly, you and I are each given the right to choose our lead out rider, the one to thrust us across the finish line. Our choice is the most important decision of our lives.

STAGE 23

The crash every rider fears

It was Friday the 7th of January, 2022. A month earlier, Leonie and Kieran Guiney had invited Jilly and me to share a few days fishing and hospitality with their family in the Marlborough Sounds at the top of the South Island of New Zealand. Curiously, Jilly turned down the kind invitation, not wanting to make the two thousand kilometre drive.

Normally I would never have considered going alone. However, I felt a compulsion to join the Guineys. It was so compelling I could not shake it. I knew that a flight would be hugely expensive and meant I couldn't take my bike, but if I drove I could easily slip my race bike into the back of my car. Voices within my head yelled that I was being extremely selfish, but I felt there was a far bigger purpose to this trip than fishing and sharing their new adventure with them, and my conscience wouldn't rest within me until I said a big yes. I had finished writing my book (or so I thought) and a few days with friends would be wonderful. I didn't know what the bigger purpose was, but I was resolute in my decision.

It was a gorgeous Friday morning when Leonie, Kieran and I clipped our shoes into the pedals of our bikes and headed out onto the quiet roads leading from Anakiwa to Havelock. The plan was to have a coffee at Havelock before returning for a day's fishing. An early morning forty kilometer ride seemed like the perfect beginning for a day in paradise.

I have no recollection of the day's events after those first thoughts, other than that I carried a strange foreboding from a dream the day before, but it seemed unrelated to bike racing.

Leonie later told me:

> "I was riding about thirty metres behind you when to my horror I saw your body lying in the middle of the road. I couldn't believe my eyes. Jumping off my bike I hurried to your side. You were unconscious, groaning and gurgling, and we both feared you were dying. There was blood coming from your mouth and nose. I prayed over you. I could see you had hit a deep pothole and had been thrown probably ten metres at about thirty-five or forty kilometres per hour, as you were in a downhill section. You had smashed into the tarmac head-first.
>
> Kieran, who had been riding in front of you, braked hard and turned to join me, staring in disbelief at your still body and vacant, bloody face. We decided it would be unwise to move you as you could have serious spinal issues. We made a call to 111 as our first duty, but then a cloud of deep concern and emotion lowered with questions and shock that had no answers. We needed a doctor immediately.
>
> Wonderfully, an Outward Bound van stopped beside me and the director of Outward Bound, who was well-versed in emergency management, assisted with blankets and advice. Shortly after that, a solo bike rider appeared, seemingly from nowhere. She was a doctor who happened to be out on a training ride. With great care she immediately examined you and cleared you to be carried carefully to a better position on the verge of the road.
>
> We stayed at your side until the ambulance arrived, though it seemed to take ages. Though you remember nothing, you seemed to come in and out of consciousness. We visited you at the Blenheim Hospital that night

but you didn't recognise us. We were deeply concerned and distressed, and again I prayed over you."

The following day, doctors at the Blenheim Hospital told me I had sustained ten broken ribs, a broken clavicle and scapula, a cracked pelvis, plus a suspected compressed section of vertebrae. The right hand side of my body was black and blue with bruising, and my shock levels were highly elevated. I wasn't sure if my heart would cope with the pain and the shock. My heart bypass of fourteen years previously kept my blood pumping, but my body felt broken, and only a drip stopped me from passing out. At seventy-seven years of age, I wondered if I would survive.

By Sunday night, my vital signs had stabilised and the staff at Blenheim Hospital arranged my transfer by Air Ambulance fixed-wing aircraft to Dunedin, where I was hurried by stretcher to the high dependence unit. Jilly surprised me that evening, arriving at my bedside full of loving comfort after her hurried drive from Queenstown to Dunedin. It was a special moment, having her hand in mine for a brief squeeze. After Jilly left the hospital, I felt a loneliness I had never felt before, and resignation flooded my heart. I wondered if I would ever see Jilly again as I sensed something big was ahead.

Sleeping through the pain wasn't easy, and being constantly awakened for bathroom visits that my medical condition demanded meant that even when I did doze off, my sleep was interrupted every hour. Nurses brought help to the bedside to save me the short hobble to the bathroom, but even so, my bones clicked together as I moved my neck, and other bones seemed to rattle around inside. Still, I was very appreciative of the love and targeted care of the nursing staff as they supported me each waking hour.

On Monday morning I had little desire for the hospital breakfast. I just wanted time by myself to reflect and pray. Laying in my room alone I noticed my life going out from me and believed my immediate journey was now taking me beyond death.

I talked to my Coach. "I am ready, I'm coming home. A long time ago you offered me the gift of eternal life, so look out, I am about to come!"

The thought of parting with life on this planet was appealing. In the past, whenever I had wandered through cemeteries, I read headstones with great interest. I decided mine would read, "I hope you are looking forward to joining me soon, as much as I am looking forward to welcoming you."

I knew Jilly would be devastated by the news of my passing but I was confident that she had the resources deep within to cope well. My grandchildren's progress in life was something that I would miss out on, but they all had parents who loved them, and I could pray for them from above. I held lightly to the assets I had accumulated over my life. They would be used wisely to help the less fortunate. I was ready!

After my chat with the Coach on the mountaintop, the spirit within me could see very clearly into the future. I had memories of hundreds of miracles and so-called coincidences that my Coach had performed throughout my life journey, but now my thoughts faded. It seemed unnecessary to worry about anything. I was left with just one thought: I would have loved to have recorded this part of my experience. I so wanted to tell the world that death for me carried no fear, but realised I couldn't as my voice and ability to write would be silenced in death. I had no idea that I would live beyond the moments ahead. I had just one last impression—that death is a one-off event that no one can escape. The grave has an insatiable appetite. Not so birth. I could see there is one death, but two births. I had experienced both births.

Expecting to slip quietly away, I shut my eyes and felt very peaceful.

My next thoughts were beyond imagination. My body felt it was floating. Blankets of love warmed me, and joy infused my spirit. Excitement joined anticipation. The stages ahead were about to take me beside still waters; I was invited to sit down at feasts, with my own nametag at my setting. I would be in the company of people with hearts overflowing with love, people I had never met. There was energy and celebration in the air, and I could only wonder why I had ever had the slightest concerns about passing. There was no time clock and therefore no hurry or agitation. My spirit had returned with energy and with a hope that was unquenchable.

When I opened my eyes and saw nurses hovering at the foot of my bed, I blinked in disbelief. How could this be true? I was still in room 4A of the Dunedin Public Hospital!

"What has happened to you, Peter?" Smiling eyes peered down at me despite mask-obscured faces. I spoke the first words that came to mind, though even as I said them I knew they were totally inadequate. "An angel has just hugged me and kissed me," I said, staring back at them. Suddenly I was overcome. I couldn't hold back the tears that filled my eyes and contorted my face.

At mid-morning on Monday the 10th of January, one day short of my seventy-eighth birthday, my room felt it had become a holy place. I could only think that the same mighty power that raised Christ from the dead two thousand years earlier had that morning been released into my spirit and kept my body alive.

My thoughts were interrupted by a cell phone, and I noticed the clock on the wall, bringing me back to the realisation that normal life had resumed. "Just ringing to say that all morning I have received phone call after phone call," Jilly said. She had no idea what she was interrupting. "So many, Peter, are saying that word had got out about the crash. Everyone is very anxious for you. Almost all told me that they are praying for you. Such love!"

"Jilly, I don't know where to begin, but the prayers of our friends have been answered in a way that I can hardly recount. I thought I was dying this morning but in the last few moments an angel kissed me." I used the same words to Jilly, that I had spoken to the nurses.

"Wow, Peter! I will ring them and tell them the good news," she replied.

With my phone again silent I got back to thinking through the experience of the morning and what it all meant. The words of this book flooded my thinking. Everything I had written stood in front of me as evidence and confirmation of the involvement of my Coach. I would now be able to write a conclusion beyond anything I could have contemplated.

My mind then turned to the title, *Born to Live*. I had been given the name of this book before I wrote one word. I had every intention to faithfully write of the many life experiences, the negative, as well as the positive. They all attested to a dynamic divine relationship and underwrote my ride in the peloton of life. I never thought that I would be granted the privilege of being able to take readers with me to look through the front gates of heaven. Briefly I had heard the music of love being played across the universe. I knew in a moment I would never be the same again. I could now wait on my Coach to give me the words that would make up these final *Born to Live* chapters.

The next days were all about rest, sleep and Panadol, but then I received an encouragement—I was ready to be relocated by ambulance to the Queenstown Hospital. This promised to be my next step towards going home. Jilly would be able to return to her own bed at Lake Hayes, just a quarter-hour drive from my bedside.

The Queenstown nursing staff welcomed me on arrival. My hospital bed, at a touch of a button, lifted my back effortlessly and allowed my sleep position to be perfect. This was a relief to my ten self-mending ribs, and shoulder bones that called for various settings during the night. Day and night, nurses attended to my every need and left me in no doubt that their work and care ethics couldn't be questioned. As I shared with them my story of life (and death?) in room 4A at the Dunedin Hospital, they were wide-eyed and amazed.

There was good news ahead. It was now Day 12, and the medical staff of the Queenstown Hospital agreed (although they seemed a little reluctant) that I could go home.

Walking out of the Queenstown Hospital, crutch-assisted, into the car park, the afternoon sun warmed my back. After days in hospital these blessings are big. It was the second-best day of my hospital life.

Jilly had made sure that the reclining passenger seat in the car was angled back to protect my aching shoulder. I found that using my left hand to lift my legs from the tarmac and into the car took pressure off my hip and groin. It turned out to be a pretty awkward but successful pain-free movement. I hoped it would be the first in my return to a normal life.

The fifteen-minute drive home to our property reminded me that the birds still sang, the mountains had lost none of their dominance, the rivers and lakes were still the lifeblood of the pastures, and the grazing livestock gave life and purpose to everything.

The word 'Home' had never sounded better.

MY THOUGHTS

The Coach prepares and equips His riders in the peloton of life to ride the mountains and push against headwinds, as well as to swoop the valleys pushed by gentle tail winds. There are reasons and divine purposes that He is fulfilling beyond the understanding of men and women. The Coach lives in the eternal, outside of time. He sees the end of all things and is aware that if we knew it all in advance, it would cause us to do everything in our power to avoid what lay ahead. And yet I believe my Coach has good and perfect plans for every rider in the *Born to Live* life.

STAGE 24

Tandem power for the asking

I don't know what time it was when sleep gave way to an excited consciousness on my first night home. At the thought of being back in my own home I was wide awake in seconds. I grabbed a crutch and made my way to a well-positioned chair in the lounge room. On the way past, the illuminated kitchen oven clock told me it was 2.45 a.m.

The floor-to-ceiling windows in our lounge room provided me with a view of the heavens; I felt I could almost reach out and touch them. I was mesmerized. The nail-clipping size of the moon that night distilled just enough light to show me an outline of Coronet Peak and the surrounding mountains. Stars hung suspended above the mountains like jewels in a treasure trove. Our tussocks stood motionless, telling me there was absence of wind. Fine wisps of tiny low-level clouds were parked for the night, stationary. But there was nothing stationary about my thoughts in that early morning hour.

My new companion, pain, tried to tug on these thoughts but wasn't successful. The awesome view, together with the peace, calmed me. Wow! Here I was, sitting at home now, alone with just my thoughts. I found it a blessing, being alive unexpectedly and still being able to laugh and wiggle my toes. Things could have been so different. Opening the door into eternal life on January the 10th would have been a very exciting end to my meaningful 28,470 days (at that time) on planet Earth. I would have been catapulted into the adventure capital of Eternity and had opportunity to talk to my Coach in person again, as well as feast in the presence of the millions gone before.

I found myself thinking about my bike ride at Havelock, the crash, and the Guiney's prayers roadside. My mind turned to the energy that had flowed into my body in the Dunedin Hospital in answer to those first prayers and others. I was surprised when my thoughts turned from that energy to atomic energy. This power was of a different sort, but it was synonymous with Havelock. Ernest Rutherford, the New Zealand scientist who pioneered the theory of splitting atoms, spent his school years just down the road from the church we attended in Havelock. His discovery had led to the building of the atomic bomb. I once read that the energy released by those bombs killed more than 200,000 Japanese people.

The thought appalled me.

An alarm bell rang in my head.

"There is energy and power with far more reach than that," my Coach whispered in my ear, "and as you know, that power is constructive, not destructive! The energy that I am talking about was released almost two thousand years ago, and is experienced by anyone who sincerely seeks. They find, and the door always opens to them."

"The evidence of this is everywhere, Coach," I replied. "I am thinking of the hospitals built, the democratic justice systems written into law based on the Judeo-Christian faith, the poor and hungry fed, the sick cared for, the incredible peace that sustained and gave hope to the millions of martyrs killed for simply believing in you, the prisoners held in chains to addictions that have been set free . . . the list is endless. And now, as I look over my own stages in the *Tour of Life* I notice your fingerprints over each stage of my life."

"True, Peter," my Coach quickly added. "The source of the power you were privileged to feel on your life journey, as well as in room 4A at the Dunedin Hospital was my Spirit. That power has been accessed and received by millions of seekers through the ages. You will meet them all one day, Pete."

The stars in the night sky suddenly seemed to glow even more strongly. It was almost like they were nodding in assent to the words of my Coach.

It all made sense. I had been the recipient of a lifetime of coaching, correction, direction and favour, but the events of the last three weeks had taken me to the coalface of the mystery of life and death itself, and I was alive to record the story.

The chiming of the vintage clock in our library told me that I had lost track of time.

I thanked my Coach for not being 'just energy'. He was much more. He had shown me again and again that He went in front and behind me on the ride of my life journey. He clearly had a cunning plan! He would never tell me of these plans in advance, as He knew my human nature would balk at them and do anything it could to evade them. Instead, He made me wait. The headwinds, steep roads and crashes were there for a reason. I would only learn from them after the event.

I was beginning to feel tired. It was now after 4 a.m. My Coach had spent some time talking to me about how He wanted me to fly with the eagles every day, or put on deer hooves so I could walk on the mountain heights.

"Pete, you wrote about riding behind the lead out rider as you approach the finish line. What does that mean for you now, as you look back over the last few weeks and beyond?" My Coach was tugging at me to write a final 'My Thoughts'.

"I said at the beginning that I felt I had been given, that day in Wellington, the fastest, lightest racing bike to ride on to make it through the Tour," I recalled.

"Yes," replied my Coach. "That was the equipment given to you, but it wasn't the power you needed to drive the pedals, or the knowledge you needed to direct the handlebars."

My Coach was absolutely correct.

"Right! That was what has always amazed me, Coach. You were continually on the race radio, and yes, sometimes (indeed, many times) my earpiece had fallen out of my ear, and you were talking alright but I wasn't listening. That was when I took a wrong turn or slid in the gravel and sometimes punctured. I paid for that big-time."

"Yes, Pete. But you always plugged the earpiece back in, even if it took awhile. It wasn't just words I was speaking through your earpiece. It was transfer of power as well."

"Coach! That is exactly what I wanted to conclude *Born to Live* with! Man, in my headstrong, impetuous moments, you saved me from hell and yet allowed those times to teach me and others life-lessons. Thankfully, I look back now and realise you were never just my Coach, talking to me on a radio. You were so much more."

I stopped to take my breath and then continued.

"I realise that the bike you gave me at age fifteen to ride on in the Tour of Life wasn't a normal racing bike. It was, in fact, the lightest, fastest carbon fibre *tandem* racing bike! It allowed the two of us to ride together!"

My Coach laughed heartily. "It took you a while to work that one out, Pete."

"So you were riding from day one on the back of my tandem?"

"Without me, Pete, you would have never made it. As you know, we climbed mountains together, and we pushed against stormy headwinds together."

My Coach was so right. He had powered me along, cleaned my wounds and bandaged me up when I fell off my bike, and from time to time reached over my shoulder to nudge my handlebars to steer me down alternative routes.

I found myself choked up with gratitude and went back to bed hoping to sleep. But the time for sleep wasn't then.

"Peter," the Coach continued. "Everyone is on a ride that eventually takes them to their final destination. All men and woman are living demonstrations of the miracle of life. Each one, surrounded by nature, are beneficiaries of a dependable and miraculous heartbeat they receive at birth. They have free access to air to breathe, to sun for heat, and to water to make their organs work. On top of that they are born with a pair of eyes that see in colour, a lifting system called strong arms, a plumbing system that removes waste, a mobility system called flexible legs, and an inbuilt repair system that swoops in to heal most of the damage that comes through accident and sickness ... and the list goes on."

I felt for my smashed shoulder and ribs. They were already healing, and comfort was slowly returning. I knew what my Coach was reminding me of—something that was working in my body at that very moment.

The first rays of dawn illuminated Coronet Peak's crown. I thanked the King of Kings and went to sleep.

The organisers of a multi-day bike race will give competitors one rest day to recuperate after seven days of riding. A masseur works on each rider each day to prepare him or her for the next stage. Below are the words that massage my mind and rest my heart every day as I ride in the peloton of life.

You have searched me, Lord, and you know me.
You know when I sit and when I rise;
you perceive my thoughts from afar.

You discern my going out and my lying down;
you are familiar with all my ways.

Before a word is on my tongue
you, Lord, know it completely.

You hem me in behind and before,
and you lay your hand upon me.

Such knowledge is too wonderful for me,
too lofty for me to attain.

Where can I go from your Spirit?
Where can I flee from your presence?

If I go up to the heavens, you are there.
if I make my bed in the depths, you are there.

If I rise on the wings of the dawn,
if I settle on the far side of the sea,

even there your hand will guide me,
your right hand will hold me fast.

If I say, "Surely the darkness will hide me
and the light become night around me,"
even the darkness will not be dark to you;
the night will shine like the day,
for darkness is as light to you.

For you created my inmost being;
you knit me together in my mother's womb.
I praise you because I am fearfully and wonderfully made;
Your works are wonderful, I know that full well.

My frame was not hidden from you
When I was made in the secret place,
When I was woven together in the depths of the earth.

Your eyes saw my unformed body;
All the days ordained for me were written in your book
before one of them came to be.

How precious to me are your thoughts, God!
How vast is the sum of them!

Were I to count them,
they would outnumber the grains of sand—
when I awake, I am still with you.

Psalm 139:1-18

ACKNOWLEDGEMENTS

In appreciation of friends who contributed with advice in the writing of the manuscript:

Dr John and Mary Clark

The Topjian family (USA)

Liesl Johnstone

Nicolette Parsons

Cheryl Fenwick

Doog Burfoot

Get in touch with Peter Yarrell at:

peter@borntolive.nz

or visit his website at www.tussockheights.co.nz

www.ingramcontent.com/pod-product-compliance
Lightning Source LLC
Chambersburg PA
CBHW051437290426
44109CB00016B/1588